Pelican Books
Studies in Social Pathology
Editor: G. M. Carstairs

THE PSYCHOTIC

Dr Andrew Crowcroft is a consultant psychiatrist
at a London post-graduate teaching hospital for
children. He was born in Hertfordshire in 1923
and has a twin brother. His mother was a Russian
aristocrat, his father a British engineer. In the
Second World War he served as a commando, and
saw much action. He qualified after the war, first in
psychology, then in medicine, and finally
specialized in both adult and child psychiatry, often
using a family approach. He has held psychiatric
appointments at three London teaching hospitals,
and has contributed articles to various professional
journals and chapters in textbooks. In 1973 he was elected a
fellow of the Royal College of Psychiatrists.
He both loves and hates writing.

Dr Crowcroft is married to a professor at the Royal
Academy of Music. He enjoys playing with his
children, hard physical work, conversation, and
world literature.

Andrew Crowcroft

The Psychotic

Understanding Madness

Penguin Books

Penguin Books Ltd, Harmondsworth, Middlesex, England
Penguin Books, 625 Madison Avenue, New York,
New York 10022, U.S.A.
Penguin Books Australia Ltd, Ringwood, Victoria, Australia
Penguin Books Canada Ltd, 2801 John Street, Markham,
Ontario, Canada L3R 1B4
Penguin Books (N.Z.) Ltd, 182–190 Wairau Road,
Auckland 10, New Zealand

First published 1967
Reprinted 1968, 1971
Reprinted with revisions 1975
Reprinted 1977

Made and printed in Great Britain by
C. Nicholls & Company Ltd
Set in Monotype Times

Contents

Editorial Foreword

During the years since the end of the Second World War, there has been a quiet revolution, both in Britain and in America, in the way in which mentally ill persons are treated. In each country new ideas were circulating and new patterns of psychiatric care were demonstrated by pioneering spirits for several years before the whole issue was publicly debated, by a Royal Commission on one side of the Atlantic, and by a Joint Commission on the other. Within two years of the publication of their reports, the recommendations of each of these Commissions were translated into legislation. In Britain, the emphasis is on 'Community Care', in the U.S.A., on 'Community Mental Health Centers': in both, steps have been taken to break down old practices which tended to segregate the mentally ill in asylums, set apart from the rest of their fellow-men.

Today, many mentally ill people are being cared for in general hospitals, in day hospitals and in the consulting rooms of their own family doctors. That this is possible is partly due to the advent of new and more effective drugs for the treatment of the psychoses; but it could not have occurred if public opinion had not shown itself ready for a new, more tolerant and more accepting attitude towards the mentally disordered.

It has been pointed out, however, that 'community care' carries with it new responsibilities for the mental patients' doctors and for their relatives, friends and neighbours. If they are neglected, or wrongly treated, mental patients can deteriorate in the community no less than they used to deteriorate in the enforced idleness of locked wards in old-fashioned mental hospitals – but with this important difference, that when they become more seriously deranged in their behaviour at home, they tend to upset other people.

The country's medical and welfare services are learning – sometimes by a process of trial and error – that quite a lot of effort must be put into the after-care of mentally ill patients who leave hospital, if they are not to relapse and require readmission. Relatives, too, are increasingly realizing that good intentions are not enough: if we are to give really effective help and support to a family member or a friend who is recuperating from serious mental illness we need to know enough about what he has been going through to enable us to treat him naturally, confidently – and appropriately.

Until quite recent times, madness has been viewed by most people with a mixture of horror and dismay. This affliction was all the more frightening because it seemed so inexplicable: the very behaviour and speech of the psychotic seemed unpredictable and incomprehensible. In fact, however, the advance of knowledge in medical psychology has already changed this situation. A great deal of the strange ideas and bizarre behaviour of mental patients can now be understood. In the case of the organic psychoses, the causes of the mental disturbance can be traced to lesions of the brain; in other major psychoses the underlying physiological processes are still very imperfectly understood, but already it is possible to show what these patients are experiencing in their thoughts and in their feelings.

In this book, Dr Crowcroft has set out to perform a threefold task. First, he gives a clear account of the phenomena of mental illness, and of the special terms which psychiatrists use to define the signs and symptoms which their patients present; secondly, he explains in non-technical language just how much – or how little – is known about the cause of each of the psychoses. His third, and perhaps most important task is to convey, with many vivid illustrations, just what it is like to be mentally ill. This is a feat of imaginative interpretation, based all the time on observations and subjective reports of patients who have lived through such experiences. He shows that madness is not after all totally alien to normal life: on the contrary, every one of us in early childhood, has fantasies as 'out of this world' as any psychotic's delusions; and all of us re-enter that illogical world from time to time, in our dreams. In other words, even very mad people are not so far removed from us as they seem to be at first sight: the problem is, of course, to understand why they seem to be immersed in dreams (if not in nightmares) even in their waking state. This book will, I believe, help its readers to have a better understanding of madness, and so to be better equipped to cope with any psychotic patients whom they may encounter. In our present-day society, one person in eight of those over the age of forty will enter a psychiatric hospital before the end of his or her life: and the great majority of these will return quite soon to resume their lives in the community, so the need for such understanding is already great and unlikely to diminish.

May 1967   G. M. CARSTAIRS

Introduction   Obstacles to Understanding

Psychiatrists today have a much clearer idea than once they had of the relevance of the attitudes of the general community to mental illness. Much is known about the effects of social forces on the insane. As both lay people and doctors are able more and more clearly to see psychosis as an 'illness', madness in ordinary life has become more acceptable. We are more likely to respond with sympathy, rather than with horror or fear, as we once did. The psychotic 'deviant', for his part, can be helped to maintain hundreds of normal social responses in his repertoire of existence. We have become very sensitive to the bad effects of only offering *custodial care* to psychotics. Social environment can contribute to therapy – aiding or thwarting recovery. Newer methods of treating psychosis aim, among other things, at avoiding *social* breakdown, which is the common cause of admission to mental hospitals. On the one hand the mental hospital itself needs to change its social function: instead of only offering a barren kind of custody it must provide therapeutic social situations. On the other hand, popular attitudes towards mental illness still need to change if our general society is not to be anti-therapeutic. We all maintain our ideas about social roles by repeated experiences of them. We do not learn them once and for all; our learning needs almost daily reinforcement. And this is true even for those who go mad. If psychotic patients are regarded as people without social meaning, except in terms of menace, if they are treated as people insensitive to their surroundings, so that they only need a greatly simplified life stripped of the subtlety and complexity of ordinary living, they become socially emptied. Continuous

The superior numbers refer to works listed by chapter on pp. 191–201.

anonymity turns people into thin shadows of the personalities they once were.

Michael Argyle[1] has noted that in small groups deviants from the norms of the group are subjected to various kinds of pressures in order to make them conform. *Rejection* is only a last resort. The majority of the members of a group of people interacting socially want deviants from its norms to fit in. Thus special social arrangements to support psychotics in the community could lead to increased public tolerance by mutual experience. The nature of 'group dynamics' suggests a pull towards adjustment through social forces. We are, of course, generalizing. The very pressure to conform can with some patients contribute to their breakdown. I believe, therefore, that there is still a need for real asylum for some psychotic patients for whom conformity, even marginal, is impossible.

The psychotic is not usually harmful in the general community, however. Here I am speaking of the community as 'us', rather than the family. In the family, unless special community services are well developed, the strain can be appalling.[2] Yet, it is not easy to change old social attitudes so that community services can operate meaningfully in a society that is itself tolerant as regards madness.

Madness is still seen as a moral problem rather than a medical one by many people; it stands as an offence against their moral code. When they say, 'He must be crazy', they mean: he is wrong, or comical, or bad, or stupid; a lunatic is some sort of perverse fool. But if – as we tend to do in the United Kingdom – we go on seeing madness as a moral problem, due to 'lack of guts', or some weird choice of a person who has a 'free will', we will go on rejecting people who are ill and whose illness came upon them as uninvited as pneumonia or appendicitis. It is difficult enough that psychotic patients often do not see themselves as ill, without our agreeing with them. We must therefore try to understand what mental illness is, although we should not underestimate the obstacles to understanding that are involved in this. Some of the problems in changing age-old prejudices concerning sickness and health emerge vividly from transcultural studies. Thus, persuading Zulu women to drink milk can be just as difficult as changing public attitudes towards mental illness. To us it seems entirely absurd that drinking milk should be forbidden to married Zulu women – until we learn a great deal about Zulu values and customs and what has powerful emotional connotations for them.[3] It is a question of feelings, of what is psycho-logical, rather than logical; a question, also, of social values, and the attitudes generated by these values.

Elaine and John Cumming have described the failure of a whole programme aimed at changing the attitudes of a Canadian community towards mental health and mental illness.[4] Despite what seemed a well thought out educational programme, there was at the end of it no detectable change in the population in its attitude towards either the mentally ill, or towards the social problem of mental illness. The community, in fact, showed resistance to the programme at times. It 'responded as if to a threat to its integrity as a functioning community'. The study showed that if anxious and hostile responses are raised in people by a provocative, emotionally loaded subject such as mental health, existing attitudes can harden rather than change.

The Cummings have traced out the usual pattern of social responses to mental illness. It seems to them that this consists of *denial*, *isolation* and *insulation*. The community they were concerned with reacted to mental illness first by denial, by acting as though the problem did not exist. If a person was so ill that it became increasingly impossible for the community to ignore him, he was isolated from the community by being hospitalized. When this had happened the whole problem could be ignored again, with the patient and the community now completely insulated from each other. There did not seem to be any point at which the community took a long, courageous, or understanding look at madness.

One of the critical factors in social rejection of the mentally ill – a trigger firing the sequence, 'He is mad, send him to hospital' – lay in *labelling*. This was 'giving a dog a bad name' with a vengeance. By labelling, the Cummings meant attaching to a person some kind of psychiatric diagnosis. As long as a person lay within the community's range of ideas of what was 'sane' or 'predictable', the community could contain the person, and if sane behaviour was expected of the deviant he seemed to find it easier to integrate, which reminds us of our earlier mention of group interaction. But once a person was thought to be *unpredictable*, society responded by rejecting him.

Having touched on some of the obstacles to understanding madness, we intend, nevertheless, to turn to understanding it. We will need to know what we mean by it, the forms it can take, and how it can be treated.

I will purposely call one of the chapters 'Labels', to show what labels really stand for. I shall not discuss 'denial, isolation and insulation' for these primitive social responses to madness derived from anxiety and hostility are inappropriate wherever there are modern mental hospitals, out-patient clinics, day hospitals, mental welfare officers, psychiatric social workers and so on. *Madness* and *lunacy* have been emotionally overcharged words for a long time. We should associate them with the words *illness*, *management* and *treatment*. In this way we will be able to cope with our anxiety when another person's behaviour seems more unpredictable than our own; thus we can be both humane and rational about the irrational, and social attitudes will begin to change.

A Royal Commission has urged fundamental changes in doctors' education with a bias in favour of the behavioural, social and psychological aspects of health.[5] The structure of the National Health Service is being greatly altered to bring a balance between hospital and community resources, the hospitals having been too dominant.[6a,6b] The Personal Social Services, which include mental health social workers, have been integrated into single integrated Local Authority Departments of Social Work.[7] In addition to all this, the principal professional organization of British psychiatry, The Royal Medico-Psychological Association, was transformed in June 1971 into the Royal College of Psychiatry, a body that guards professional standards, sets its own examinations, and has an equal voice with all other medical specialities.[8] A more realistic idea of the cost of better mental health services, both in the short[9] and longer term[10] is being formed. The psychiatric needs of the population are being better assessed and predicted statistically, though not without controversy.[11] The severe shortage of psychiatric nurses is at least recognized, if it has yet to be corrected.[12]

Part One

Part One

1 Normal, Neurotic, Psychotic

Physical illnesses, particularly ones caused by germs, have yielded on the whole to scientific research. Physicians and surgeons look determinedly beyond the patient's symptoms to make their diagnoses. Of course, physical medicine still has many problems. Yet they seem to be of the same nature as those in which traditional scientific research has eventually been successful. From this kind of understanding will come cure.

However, in psychiatry little of this way of looking at disease has yet borne real fruit. The laboratory still has to help us to make most of our diagnoses. Our classifying systems have yet to be based on causes in the sense of the recognition of the diseased material parts of people.

The organ of special interest might seem to be the brain. Our interest might appear to be the central nervous system. However, neurology and psychiatry are different subjects. The former bases itself on the orthodox view of physical medicine. It is organic. Psychiatry, on the other hand, is not (with some exceptions which we will consider). It is interesting to note that Freud himself began in neurology, even making original contributions to the subject.[1] Ackerknecht, in his excellent short history of psychiatry,[2] includes a chapter entitled 'From Neurology to Psychoanalysis', and shows how in the last two decades of the nineteenth century progress in psychiatry came from the contributions of a series of often very great neurologists who gave up neurology in any real sense in so far as they made contributions to psychiatry. The problem is one of *trying to understand and classify symptoms, not causes in the material sense.*

And so there is, right from the beginning, a profound difference between psychiatry and general medicine. There is also the problem of the language used by psychiatrists. It is not always even a standard language. This in itself is perhaps to be criticized, and many of the different descriptive systems in psychiatry should be largely reduced to one by careful definitions. It is not, however, enough to say that, 'The general physician and the neurologist regard physical manifestations as a prime focus of interest, and it is really only in this rather unimportant feature that they distinguish themselves from the psychiatrist.'[3] All major psychiatric textbooks classify psychiatric illness by psychological criteria, not by physical ones. Those who have tried the naming methods of 'proper medicine' can be relegated to the historical review section in a comprehensive textbook.[4]

This does not mean to say that basic somatic research in, say, biochemistry or neurology is wrong-headed. It is just that it has yet to achieve practical results which can benefit psychiatric patients or add to our understanding of them.[5,6] Neither does it mean that certain physical methods of treatment do not work. Above all it does not imply that scientific method is irrelevant to psychiatry.

*

We have said that psychiatry classifies by symptoms. Symptoms are what one describes when asked 'What are you complaining of?'* In attempting to classify psychiatric symptoms we find, apparently, only a few broad types of mental disorders. Let us first examine the terms *neurosis* (or 'psychoneurosis') and *psychosis*. These generally refer to very different kinds of disturbance. The simplest classification of neuroses is one which includes *anxiety states, hysteria* and the *obsessional neurosis*. I want to characterize neurotic illnesses briefly, and then point out how neuroses differ from psychoses, turning to examine the psychoses in detail in the next chapter.

An anxiety state is one in which there is a very high level of experienced fear, and any physical symptoms seem to be the outcome of this. Here is a simple example of such a state:

---

* To the complaints are added the impression given by the person by the way he describes things, by his behaviour, and how all this compares with what one knows of his life as it appears to us. This of course involves the psychiatrist in value judgements.

Dead British and German soldiers still sprawled awkwardly on the ground near the beaches. Some of their bodies were mercifully hidden by the heavy-headed, arching golden wheat, in the fields of June.

Lofty sweated even though cold rain fell. His rifle trembled in his shaking hands. He could not stay still, but in the failing light kept abruptly changing his place in the slit trench. His comrades were rapidly losing all morale, as Lofty said over and over again, 'They're coming, they're coming, they're coming,' in a voice thick with fear. For the others, Normandy was their baptism of fire. For Lofty, it came after North Africa and Italy, and he was no longer supported by the illusion of it-cannot-happen-to-me.

A clinician would have noted dilated pupils, a rapid pulse and other signs that the in-built 'flight or fight' mechanisms in this soldier had become useless caricatures of their normal selves. Lofty, however, remains basically himself. He is the same person he was before D-day, only a very frightened version. He is a simple example. In the less dramatic environments of peace, anxiety states can be seen in which the anxiety, from the patient's point of view, is 'objectless', even though to people familiar with his life situation, there appear to be obvious connexions between his symptoms and his situation. He may only complain of the physical sensations which go with great fear. He may be tense and irritable; he is constantly apprehensive, and so often exhausted. Such an emotional strain makes concentration difficult and memory unreliable. With anxious dreams, he may well wonder if he is going mad, though he is not.

Hysteria has no short definition. There is, on the one hand, the hysterical character, and on the other, hysterical symptoms. Karl Jaspers said the former is a person who

needs to appear in his own eyes and those of others more than he actually is, to experience more than he is capable of experiencing. In place of genuine, spontaneous experience, naturally expressed, there appears a spurious, theatrical and forced experience, not consciously so, but arising from his ability, the true hysterical attribute, to live entirely on his own stage and for the moment identifying himself entirely with his role ...

Hysterical symptoms may be physical (conversion hysteria) or mental. Almost any symptom of true physical disease may be imitated in hysteria – anaesthesia of some part of the body, paralysis, tremors, vomiting or even fits. The commonest symptoms are 'blackouts' or bodily pain. The form of the imitation of physical disease is, of course, usually an essentially lay one. The mental symptoms can include amnesia, and disturbances of consciousness. Cases of *multiple personality*, in which a person acts as if he were a different person on different occasions, are hysterical; they are also extremely rare.

The basic mechanism in hysteria is *dissociation*. It represents, in a way, a flight into illness, for unconscious gain. For example:

The young woman appeared quite calm at the case conference. Medical students examined her paralysed feet and asked her questions. No, she had no worries. She was sure her troubles followed treatment at such and such a hospital for some minor complaint. She was equally sure there was an operation that could make her feet better.

In fact, the paralysis corresponded with no known physical illness. It took many months of psychotherapy before this patient could acknowledge parts of herself that filled her with guilt and shame. She came from a family devoted to a narrow religious sect, in which all things sexual were dirty and not even to be thought of. And so, when sexually aroused by an attempt to rape her, she *dissociated* herself from the incident. That is to say, she broke off all conscious memory of it, repressed it. Her symptom – the paralysed feet – symbolized many things to her unconsciously. That is, the symptom was 'over-determined'. It represented a compromise between the expression of an instinctual gratification, and its prohibition. With crippled feet she could not be blamed for what happened. The emotions felt in her conflict were now all underground, and so she appeared calm. Once neglected in her emotionally chaotic family, she was now its pathetic star.

Obsessional neurosis is marked by an overriding feeling of compulsion. At the same time, the obsessive person feels he should resist his compulsions and knows that they interfere with ordinary life. The rather rigid, fastidious, hardworking and conscientious individual has an obsessional personality, which we would not call a neurosis. However, this kind of personality can sometimes be the pre-morbid personality of an obsessional neurotic, who may have been an obstinate, irritable, morose kind of person, or a vacillating, submissive, uncertain one; in any case, the previous personality was beset with inner insecurities. Behind its correct and prudish manner could be found a rather perverse sexuality. The overt obsessional behaviour seems to be an over-compensation for this. Obsessional ideas are expiatory, an attempt to overcome, by a kind of mental magic, deeper distress.

In such personalities, prone to self-reproach, perfectionist, yet often indecisive, heightened emotional stress gives rise to ideas and fears of a neurotic intensity. Compulsions to step over cracks between paving stones, to touch wood for luck, the tune that keeps going round in our heads, are all familiar examples of obsessional acts or thoughts that most of us have experienced some time, usually in childhood. We can imagine, therefore, how the intensification or exaggeration of such experience can become a neurosis. States of indecision or doubt can balloon into a *folie de doute*, driving a woman to return again and again to see if gas taps are turned off, or doors locked. Absurdly usual things terrify. Odd habits become elaborated into complex rituals so time-consuming that perhaps nothing else can be done; when unravelled, these fantastic rituals can be seen as heavily disguised self-reproaches.

It can be extremely difficult to differentiate a severe neurosis from a psychosis, but there are some general distinctions. A neurosis signifies mental conflict. It reflects inner tensions and maladapted responses to stress. For example, some neurotics may have a recurrent pattern of reaction which is responsible for unsatisfactory relationships with other people. The neurotic is either unconscious of his internal conflict, or does not connect it with his symptoms. His symptoms may therefore appear irrational to him and to us. Yet what seems mysterious often becomes logical again, and understandable, if we can connect enough of his feelings to his thoughts. And as we do so, we see that many physically healthy, even highly intelligent adults can be totally unaware of some of their own feelings. Without greatly committing ourselves to any particular school of psychiatry, we can say that the confused interpersonal relationships of the neurotic are referrable to his earlier life. For him some of 'the past is not past'. He acts in certain situations as though they were earlier situations with which he had also failed to come to terms realistically. The neurotic can therefore show unusual emotional reactions but, while we may occasionally think he is 'difficult', we do not usually think he is mad. Anxiety-prone, obsessional, or whatever, he shares our world, he acts as though reality is the same for him as for anyone else. This is not so in the case of the psychotic:

She was a gaunt woman and the wasting of her face made her dark eyes huge. There was already a mysterious light in them as she leaned forward and said she was in her neighbours' power. An intelligent face, yet she had cigarette ash over a new torn coat. She was intelligent, yet she believed her neighbours used cosmic rays to torture her. Their voices plotting against her ran through her head even as she spoke of them. Her own voice was curiously dead and unemotional. She spoke of horror as though unhorrified. [A schizophrenic.]

Or consider Billy:

He is huge for his age. A spotty adolescent, he stands in the hospital corridor. His mother stands close to him. She is moving her body slowly, seductively, as she speaks to him and he seems to respond to this, some-how aroused. Yet his mother is jabbing her finger into his chest and, in a voice quivering with anger, denounces him for wearing his over-coat on such a warm day. Billy is perplexed, glancing at the accusing finger, and beyond it to his mother herself. He too hears voices that are not there, as another part of his perplexed agony. We see him loving and hating this woman at the same time. Or rather we see he does not know if he loves or hates. He licks his lips and backs to the wall. [Billy also is mad.]

There are many kinds of morbid fears, intrusive thoughts or acts, bodily disturbances or even curious transitory mental states, affecting the memory, or causing trances, which are classed as neurotic symptoms. The individual experiencing any of these recognizes that they are abnormal, even though their meaning baffles him. He may wonder if he is physically ill, or even believe that he is. Certainly psychological pain hurts as much as pain of organic origin. However, the fact that he realizes something is wrong shows that he still has insight into himself which the psychotic does not. The psychotic may not realize that his experiences are markedly different from those of other people, or even from his own before he became ill.

A neurosis is a minor illness compared to the major impact of a psychotic attack. This is because only a part of the personality is involved in a neurotic reaction, whereas in psychosis, the whole personality is involved, as in this puerperal psychosis:

The woman knelt, praying aloud in the middle of the teashop. She was very Irish, but through her brogue the story of her miscarriage came tumbling out, her subsequent guilt feelings, her unworthiness, the terrible punishment she deserved and was therefore receiving. The themes of despairing womanhood, Catholicism, death and torture, emerged again and again. Those seated nearest her were acutely embarrassed. No one, however, looked at her, or spoke a word. The manageress came and led her away through the crowded teashop.

The character of reality remains the same for a neurotic. The very nature of reality changes for the psychotic, terrifying as such a change sounds. Terrifying it can be, too, for the person to whom it happens. And since reality changes, there are also very marked changes in behaviour. Thus the neurotic lives in our world, partly or almost wholly; a psychotic is not only out of his mind, but also out of our world.

If we regard mental illnesses as regressions, a slipping or crashing back to early stages of development, only the very severe neuroses begin to approach the primitive levels of mental experience commonly found in the psychotic. Thus language, the 'symbolizing function and the latest developed function for social adaptation', which is often disturbed in a major illness, is not affected in neurosis.[4]

'I always find it uncanny when I can't understand someone in terms of myself,' says Freud.[1] We do not have a problem of the uncanny with the neurotic. He is fairly close to normality and we are relatively tolerant of his symptoms because of the very similarity between himself and ourselves. Why does he make such heavy weather of things, we may ask, or even, why doesn't he pull himself together? His personality can seem so normal apart from his symptoms that in some instances we describe him quite accurately as only having problems with certain of his attitudes.

On the other hand, it is with some rather vague idea of neurosis in mind that many of us cheerfully admit that nowadays 'nobody is normal'. The psychotic's behaviour, on the other hand, is very far from everyday life. He makes poor contact with others and is withdrawn, living in a world of his own. The glimpses he shows us of his world, as he answers voices we cannot hear, or suffers from punishments we do not understand, frighten us.

We mentioned earlier the question of the language used by psychiatrists. Let us define some descriptive terms which different authors sometimes use in different senses. As we do so, perhaps we will see how these terms can increase our understanding of madness.

The *ego* – the *me* – is an organized part of the mind and is largely conscious. It is therefore in touch with reality. Its ideas of reality are transmitted to it by the senses, and it has ready access to many of our memories. It is, in a way, our rational conscious centre. It arises and develops out of our unconscious minds. In normal development under the influence of the real external world it gains increasing control over the barbaric instinctual forces which constitute the unconscious part of the mind. This view of mind is nothing if not dynamic and it sees human instinctual forces, or drives, as constantly trying to express themselves, as forces grasping hard for gratification here and now, like a small child.

The *id* is a technical word for the unconscious mind, which consists of a mass of primitive drives. Often the rather dated word 'instincts' is used to name these drives.

Unconscious ideas in the id are not rationally related one to another, and phantasies which are polar opposites in terms of impulse or meaning can jostle side by side, or even coalesce in paradox. There is no time, logic, or structure; no shame, social awareness, or regret. The id learns nothing and forgets nothing. It is the world before civilization, filled with the images of primitive creation and destruction. If this chaotic side of ourselves threatens to break into *awareness* and into behaviour, we experience unpleasant anxiety. We can, however, act with unconscious motivation, unaware of the origins of an impulse. And since we so easily rationalize, the conscious reasons we devise for such acts prevent us from experiencing anxiety. The ego thus operates between a large, unknown, unconscious part of ourselves, and the outside world.

We are all linked to our environment by the way we are made, by our special senses – our eyes and ears, our sense of touch and so on. The world is a meaningful place to us, and one in which we make emotional attachments. We are guided through the situations we find ourselves in not only by our conscious and unconscious emotional needs, but also by *anxiety*, the ordinary response to stress. This emotional response to danger helps us to survive and makes biological sense. Anxiety has been called 'fear spread thin'. It is reasonable to worry whether children are old enough to cross a road safely, or whether we are earning enough to pay our bills. Anxieties like these make us more alert, and change our behaviour usefully. If we can, we deal with the situation, and the unpleasant feeling of anxiety dies away. This is anxiety operating normally.

Situations which provoke anxiety in us in a fairly normal way are legion. Some of these situations would provoke anxiety in anybody. Others can be very personal and specific. Thus most of us would have the same sort of feelings on finding a lion in the back garden. On the other hand, anxieties arising from, say, a threatened loss of love, or from abandonment, emerge from interpersonal relationships that can be extremely complex and in detail almost unique. Yet, if we know the detail, the anxiety seems logical and the behaviour arising in response to the anxiety reasonable, or at least understandable.

The fact that we all know what anxiety is like makes it easier to know how another person may be feeling and, in particular, makes it possible to reach out from our everyday imaginations towards the inner experience of the neurotic. For he reacts to the same kind of events as we do, even if he does so to excess, or in a way that will not really help him deal with the cause of his anxiety.

Anxiety is an unpleasant experience, whether arising in the neurotic or psychotic personality, or in a so-called normal one. For this reason, the ego has certain defences against it. It is not relevant to go into detail about these defences here – repression, regression and so on – as they are very lucidly and appropriately described elsewhere.[7] The point I wish to make is that the ego is a complex structure, and its defences can be either strong or weak.

It is in terms of *ego strength* that the difference between a neurotic and a psychotic can be seen most clearly. A well organized ego can withstand a great deal of anxiety, wherever the threat arises. A weak ego may succumb, becoming disorganized and 'fragmented' (see page 82). In doing so, the unconscious forces previously held back burst into consciousness. The psychotic then knows his own unconscious and is unable to deal adequately with its impulses, or with the anxiety that these impulses provoke in him. He is also ill-equipped to deal with the vagaries of his outer world. Relationships with other people suffer, since it is through the ego that these relationships are carried on. More dramatically, the essential and reassuring links with generally accepted reality are broken.

None of this happens in neurosis, unless it is very malignant. The neurotic ego holds out. The defences against anxiety work. The very existence of symptoms in a neurosis can be interpreted as a partially successful means of protection against experiencing anxiety.[8] Neurosis is a result of conflict between the individual and society, and of conflicts within the individual, but the neurosis is itself evidence of the continuity of the main structures of the personality. There is no final feeling of alienation between normality and neurosis.

If we think of the ego as a structure existing in relationship to other people, to the outside world, and to the total self, we can say that it has a boundary. Where the ego ends, the inner and outer worlds begin. The idea of an 'ego-boundary'[9] is not only clinically useful, it is another bridge to understanding mad people – curiously enough, by remembering love. The unity of lovers as described by an artist in paint, stone or words shows us that the act of loving can lead normal people into feeling states where familiar personal identity is lost, and with it the ego-boundary.

He had started towards the Brady party when he saw Kathleen sitting in the middle of a long white table, alone.

Immediately things changed. As he walked towards her, the people shrank back against the walls till they were only murals; the white table lengthened and became an altar where the priestess sat alone. Vitality swelled up in him, and he could have stood a long time across the table from her, looking and smiling.

The incumbents of the table were crawling back – Stahr and Kathleen danced.

When she came close, his several visions of her blurred; she was momentarily unreal. Usually a girl's skull made her real, but not this time – Stahr continued to be dazzled as they danced out along the floor – to the last edge, where they stepped through a mirror into another dance with new dancers whose faces were familiar but nothing more.[10]

This, then, is being 'madly' in love.

*

To sum up, a psychotic is a person who has very severe problems in relating to his environment and other people. A neurotic shares our kind of existence even if it seems more difficult for him. For the psychotic, on the other hand, phantasy can often seem fact. In other words, the facts of the reality of his world differ profoundly from our own. His contact with what we call reality appears to us poorer than our own. He seems generally not to notice the difference between his world and ours, and we say, therefore, that he lacks insight. The disorganization of his mind, which is his illness, is far worse than that of a neurotic and may be of a different kind. Certainly, psychotic experiences are infinitely more primitive than neurotic ones.

There are several varieties of psychotic illness. Let us now see what they are, even if our classification of people and their ills can, perhaps, never be perfect.

Labels

It has become a cliché among some psychiatrists to talk disparagingly of 'mere labelling'. They mean by this that simply giving a name to an illness does not help the patient, that a name does not necessarily explain anything. I accept these views, but this does not mean that we must not use labels at all. From the practical point of view alone – in the organization and planning of a Mental Health Service, and in anticipating the Service's future needs – we need to know how many people are seriously mentally handicapped in the community and also what sort of handicap they have. These facts are obviously necessary if we are to know what kind of different treatment facilities to provide for people with very different needs. From a theoretical point of view, perhaps, people can be graded, from 'normal enough' to neurotic, and from neurotic through to psychotic. Nevertheless, a difference in degree can amount to a difference in kind. The everyday world is not a chaotic asylum, odd though many of us may be at times. There is a difference between having a good cry and feeling better for it, and having a good cry and then killing yourself; or between feeling you haven't very nice neighbours, and believing they are out to poison you. There is a difference between coping, and being unable to cope. A mere fragment of psychotic behaviour or experience can be more weird or frightening than many of the problems of a neurotic kind.

In our attempts to define true madness we sometimes use very subjective terms. The commoner names and descriptions of mental illnesses are based on more objective criteria – observed behaviour. When we consider psychosis as a cultural deviation we will see the limits of this 'objectivity'. It is usual to divide up the psychoses into the *Organic Psychoses*, which are mental disorders in which physical factors are of major importance, and *Functional Psychoses*, where no organic changes can be indicted causally. Acute and chronic confusional states are examples of the former group; the *Affective Psychoses* and *Schizophrenia* are important illnesses belonging to the latter.

The Affective Psychoses – Affective Reaction Types – Manic-Depressive Psychosis

These names are given to a group of mental disorders in which the basic upset is one of the *emotions* (affect). Individuals experiencing this type of illness vary in their mood from one time to another. For a period they are in a state of extreme elation; at another time they are profoundly depressed. This variation from cheerfulness to sadness is out of all proportion to any obvious variance in the patient's life-situation. Indeed, it may seem at odds with their opportunities. All their other symptoms seem secondary to exaggerated elation (or mania) or profound sadness. For this reason Kraepelin called the condition manic-depressive insanity.[1]

Leonard Woolf wrote of his wife, Virginia Woolf:

... then suddenly the headache, the sleeplessness, the racing thoughts would become intense and it might be several weeks before she could begin again to live a normal life. But four times in her life the symptoms would not go and she passed across the border which divides what we call insanity from sanity ... there were two distinct stages which are technically called manic-depressive. In the manic stage she was extremely excited; the mind raced; she talked volubly and, at the height of the attack, incoherently.... During the depressive stage all her thoughts and emotions were the exact opposite of what they had been in the manic stage. She was in the depths of melancholia and despair; she scarcely spoke; refused to eat; refused to believe that she was ill and insisted that her condition was due to her own guilt; at the height of this stage she tried to commit suicide, in the 1895 attack, by jumping out of a window, in 1915 by taking an overdose of Veronal; in 1941 she drowned herself in the river Ouse ...

There were moments or periods during her illness, particularly in the excited stage, when she was what could be called 'raving mad' and her thoughts and speech became completely uncoordinated, and she had no contact with reality. Except for these periods, she remained all through her illness, even when most insane, terribly sane in three-quarters of her mind. She believed, for instance, that she was not ill, that her symptoms were due to her own 'faults'...[2]

Many of the more important features of the disorder are depicted in this quotation.

Three main characteristics of this psychosis are that the basic disturbance is of the *feelings*, that this disturbance is *periodic* and that *recovery from an attack leaves a personality entirely unimpaired*. The last point is particularly important to remember when we come to consider the social effects of psychoses.

Manic-depressive psychosis usually appears first between the ages of twenty and thirty-five, and it is commoner among women than men.* Milder versions of the adult psychosis can be found, forming a graded series between the slight changes of predominating mood that so many nearly normal people experience, and the full-blown psychotic picture. A *cyclothymic temperament* has been described as a non-psychotic half-way house between normality and psychosis. A person having such a temperament experiences quite pronounced changes of predominating mood. There are long periods in their lives when they are rather morose, silent and relatively unproductive. Then they swing into a phase of good humour when they are full of energy and drive. Some manic-depressives appear to have had a cyclothymic temperament before becoming psychotic. Another feature often found associated with both this psychosis and with cyclothymia is a particular physique, a thick-set, rounded bodily configuration, the so-called *pyknic build*.

It must be understood that psychotic feelings of depression have the quality of the most extreme despair: the despair that can lead to suicide. Of the five or six thousand people who commit suicide in the United Kingdom each year, a large proportion suffer from an affective disorder. If untreated, these illnesses can

*For the sake of completeness, we should note that infants and children can become severely depressed. In a psychodynamic sense, that is to say in terms of inner fantasies, children can have manic-depressive experiences. Drs Anthony and Scott have shown in a very interesting paper how the classical depressive psychosis of adult life does not appear in childhood with identical features. They explain how this 'psychodynamic psychosis' of childhood can become 'extraverted' at puberty, showing the features found in the adult's illness.[3]

also be of great duration, lasting for years. It would have been very depressing to write of depression thirty or forty years ago, when there was little or nothing that could be done to end or shorten the illness. Psychotherapy did exist but there were even fewer psychotherapists than now; and in any case not by any means all depressed patients can be cured by psychotherapy.

However, the majority of depressives can now be very effectively treated. The peculiar problem of this condition stems from one of its symptoms: the patient himself has, as part of his illness, no insight into his illness. He does not see himself as ill, and he also has an overwhelming sense of guilt. In other words, he may well view his condition as moral rather than medical. He will not seek treatment for his symptoms, because he thinks of himself as bad rather than mad. He feels that he is 'only getting what he deserves'. His guilt thus bars him from seeking help. For this reason it is important that people in the community should learn to recognize abnormal depressive reactions for what they are. It is not hard to imagine how difficult it can be to live with a perpetually gloomy, slowed-up husband or wife. Yet buried in such an individual, quite intact, is a healthy person. Despite the complexity and apparent permanence of the depressed mood, modern treatments are very effective.

Kraepelin, whose labels remain the most widely used in the world, includes under the manic-depressive heading isolated attacks of depression or of mania. He also includes the depressions of later life, the *Involutional Melancholias*.

Depressions are sometimes classified as *endogenous* or *exogenous* ('neurotic' or 'reactive'). They are called endogenous when environmental factors are thought to be insufficient to account for the severity of the disease. This contrasts with the exogenous, or reactive depressions, where the reasons for the individual to be depressed are more obvious, such as bereavement or sudden poverty. Many psychiatrists think that no real distinction can be made between endogenous and exogenous depressions,[4] and that 'reactive' factors are always present, that is to say, understandable features in the patient's environment that contribute to his illness. It is my own view that depressive illnesses arise out of a complexity of interpersonal relationships and needs; I also believe that depressions develop in people who are already vulnerable, and not completely 'out of the blue'. The trigger itself may seem insignificant to the onlooker. The gun that fires was cocked long since.

For practical purposes, however, it is important to try to distinguish between different types of depression. This is not only because this can be a guide to the risk of suicide involved, but also because it can lead to the most efficient form of treatment.

In a severe endogenous depression patients look as they feel, bowed down by despair, older than their years, their faces haggard with melancholy. They are so slowed up physically and mentally that a stranger might mistake their *psychomotor retardation* for stupidity. Their voices are monotonous, and they act as though speaking or moving, or even just living were a huge burden to them. They feel constantly tired and heavy, as their sleep leaves them entirely unrefreshed. They tend to wake very early, and it is in the mornings that they feel most depressed. As the day passes the mood may lighten. Many of these patients find insomnia one of their worst symptoms and an unrewarding night brings them back to another grim morning. They are full of self-accusation and lack all hope. Thinking is unrealistic to a delusional degree; they imagine that they have caused enormous damage to those they love and perhaps to the world. They may be unable to cry even though they wish to. If they do so it leads to no purging of the emotions. It is hopeless crying. Yet for all this the severely depressed person can experience feelings of anger. The physical side of this illness includes a loss of sexual desire: a depressed man may complain only of his impotence if he seeks medical help. In addition to a loss of libido, an endogenously depressed woman may have scanty menstrual periods, or none at all. An important symptom is an extreme loss of appetite leading to loss of weight, which can be very severe, and to constipation from low food intake. Hypochondriacal symptoms, such as believing parts of the gut are missing, or that some part of the body is dead and rotting, may be present. A preoccupation with such imaginary bodily ailments is sometimes more prominent in the patient's mind than his feelings of depression. These have been called 'masked depressions' or 'depressive equivalents'. The degree of depression may nevertheless be very severe, and the patient may be as much a suicide risk as one in whom the mood is obvious.

Although their slowing-down may make them appear dull-witted, depressed patients do not suffer from intellectual impairment. Consciousness is clear, but the endogenously depressed become very egocentric; the environment holds much less interest for them than it did when they were well. Because of this ego-centricity and the enormous effort that doing anything demands from them, they do less and less, withdrawing from old recreations and perhaps avoiding old friends. While feelings of depression are predominant, there is also an overwhelming sense of guilt, which leads to savage self-accusations, apprehensiveness, and gloomy ideas of impending punishment or disaster. There are several variants of endogenous depression. On the one hand the degree of psychomotor retardation can be so extreme as to produce a *depressive stupor;* on the other hand, particularly in older patients, instead of retardation there can be an immensely distressing restlessness, with extreme anxiety, and persecutory as well as depressive ideas. Because he is so active, a patient suffering from *Agitated Depression*, as this is called, is in greater danger from his self-destructive impulses than a severely retarded patient.

Involutional Melancholia, as the name implies, appears in people 'past middle age' and it resembles agitated depression. That is to say, the patient does not show psychomotor retardation. He often expresses grotesque hypochondriacal ideas, and, as part of the morbid anxiety he feels, can despairingly complain of feelings of unreality and of emptiness, as though he were devastated by some huge sense of loss. His prepsychotic personality often seems to have been an obsessional one. He was a conscientious, rather tense and worrying sort of person, with a lot of drive. Then, coinciding with middle age, some extra worry arises – financial strain, the death of a relative, or the break-up of the family – and he gradually breaks down into a state of exaggerated remorse, dangerous to himself because of his suicidal impulses and his lack of insight into the unreality of the emotional world he now lives in.

Since environmental factors may be found relevant in both endogenous and exogenous depressions, these are usually differentiated from one another on other grounds. Exogenous or reactive depressions (pathological grief reactions to easily understandable stresses) are characterized by tension and anxiety being more prominent than other features. Depressive feelings themselves are worse in the latter part of the day, rather than on waking; it is understandable that getting off to sleep, when the mood is at its worst, is the problem, rather than early waking. Indeed, over-sleeping in the morning may be a difficulty, rather than early waking, as though the patient feared to face the day. The re-actively depressed share with the endogenously depressed a chronic feeling of tiredness; psychosomatic symptoms are com-mon in both. While, as we have seen, the endogenously depressed are guilt-ridden, and blame themselves for everything, the patient with a reactive depression more often tends to blame other people for the way he feels. His depression builds up slowly and clears in time, when the precipitating factors have gone. Endogenous depressions tend to have a sudden onset; they also remit spon-taneously, leaving the patient's personality unimpaired. But this may only be after weeks, months or years of suffering, unless treatment is sought.

Depressive symptoms can be seen in a variety of organic brain diseases. They are, for example, common as part of *arterio-sclerotic dementia*, which is caused by the 'hardening of the arteries' of the brain. There are several other symptoms in this illness which we will touch on in describing the senile psychoses. In old age generally, depressive illnesses are common, and are as treatable as at any other age. Depressions from the fifties onwards, however, are increasingly dangerous from the point of view of the risk of suicide. A variety of infections can produce depressive reactions, and severe depressions have also sometimes followed the use of certain drugs, such as rauwolfia, a drug used in the treatment of hypertension.

For convenience, we have considered the main features and varieties of depression together. However, in manic-depressive psychosis, mania or depression can appear either alone, or alternating with one another. In mania the mood is one of elation. This elation is just as pathological and unrelated to the patient's real life situation as a psychotic depression. Manic phases may alternate with depressive ones in an irregular way, but in some patients periodic swings from one state to another can keep their form and regularity almost exactly for years. The elated mood is extremely unstable. That is to say, while the patient feels 'on top of the world', or 'master of all he surveys', his emotions range rapidly through joy, sorrow, anger or irritability. He is over-driven both physically and mentally and like a young child cannot bear frustration, or the postponement of pleasure. He may be joyously, infectiously happy one moment, but if he is denied some trivial request he loses his temper. In mania, as in psychotic depression, the patient has no insight, and does not see himself as ill. On the contrary, he feels that his life has become immensely intensified and that he has achieved freedom from all the petty restraints that once enchained him. While depressed, he felt emptied, devastated and guilt-ridden. Now he feels enriched, masterful and guiltless. Yet, like the depressed person, he does not notice his egocentricity, or the effects of his unnatural mood upon his interpersonal relations; they have importance to him only in so far as he can get what he wants out of them.

Thought as well as behaviour reflects the elated mood. The manic patient talks quickly and when 'very high' his speech becomes a *flight of ideas*, where words are linked by rhymes and puns, or by their mere sounds. The effect can be very witty and, as it is so uninhibited, very salacious. However, speech never reaches the private, socially meaningless quality of the *speech disorder* that can be found in schizophrenia. The manic patient is over-active and restless, doing everything at the top of his voice. He may be too busy with too many things to complete any single task, so that he even neglects to eat properly and cannot settle down to sleep. As ordinary social mores have become unimportant to him, he may become involved in sexual assaults, or indecent exposure. He may develop what older books call 'degraded habits' – soiling himself, or smearing his faeces round the room, or in a frustrated moment breaking anything he pleases. I dislike the word 'degraded' myself, as it has too many moral overtones. These features are in fact 'regressed' ones, and reflect the essentially infantile nature of the patient's emotional repertoire while ill.

There are several varieties of mania, ranging from a mild version, *hypomania*, through to *hyperacute mania*, commonly known as 'brain fever'. In the very severe forms behavioural

coherence is entirely lost, and hallucinations and delusions –
which are words we will define later – are common.

Attacks of mania, like attacks of endogenous depression, tend
to come on suddenly. For the first few days a person may feel
irritable and have insomnia. In some cases he may at first be even
quite depressed. Then rapidly the full manic picture which we have
described develops. Any of the forms of mania can switch abruptly
into more or less acute versions, or into a depressive psychosis.

Chronic mania stands somewhat apart from the 'graded series'
of hypomania to hypermania. It tends to appear first later in life
than other manias, about the same time as involutional melancholias. Chronic mania can be very persistent, as its name implies,
and without treatment it can run on for years. Although generally
fairly mild, it can swing at times into acute forms, or into depression.

A mild hypomania may be an asset in making one's way in the
world. The characteristic wit and tireless energy, the abundance
of ideas, could be thought special gifts. But the domineering,
irritable manner of a manic patient lacking insight into his own
condition obviously makes him a difficult person to live with. At
the higher levels of mania the nagging, aggressiveness, and in-
consistency of such a person are socially exhausting. He monopo-
lizes conversation, starts what he cannot finish, is intolerant of
opposition and outstays his welcome. In acute mania, he can
obviously no longer cope with day-to-day living. Again, however,
contemporary treatments can be very effective.

The Schizophrenias – Schizophrenic Reaction Types

We should use the plural, at least once, as a reminder that
Bleuler,[5] in coining the term, thought the name might cover more
than one kind of illness. As with the affective psychoses, the
original grouping together of several symptoms into one illness
was the work of Kraepelin. His name for the group was 'dementia
praecox'. Bleuler changed the term, since patients do not necessarily become demented, nor are they always young when they
fall ill. We will consider schizophrenia in more detail in a moment,
but before doing so, we must clear up what seems to be a widespread misconception. It is often mistakenly thought that

schizophrenia means 'split mind' or 'multiple personality'. This is a confusion of schizophrenia with hysteria. In our earlier contrasting of neurotic and psychotic disorders, we noted that multiple personality – 'split mind', or 'double personality' – is an extremely rare form of hysteria. In it, the dissociation mechanism characteristic of hysteria, the separating of different parts of the personality, becomes so extensive that one or another separate part is able to appear, superficially, as an alternate, whole personality in its own right. The classical literary example of this hysterical condition is Dr Jekyll and Mr Hyde.

The confusion between 'split mind' and multiple personality on the one hand, and schizophrenia on the other, doubtless arises from the fact that the word 'schizophrenia' means 'splitting of mind'. However, Bleuler, influenced in his terminology by association psychology, wished to convey a much more profound disruption of mind than dissociation: the basis of schizophrenia is a splitting within thinking and feeling themselves, between, for example, internal and external perception, a loosening in the association of ideas, which leads to a deep disturbance of both thought and feelings, and thus to a disorder of the whole personality.

Schizophrenia develops between puberty and the forties; it affects both sexes equally. It consists of a severe disturbance of thinking, behaviour and feelings, and an increasing withdrawal of interest from the environment; the patient is preoccupied with phantasy rather than reality, and one often finds delusions and hallucinations. It is often a progressive illness, even though its course may be remittent; schizophrenics, therefore, make up the largest section of the chronic group of the mentally disordered. Despite modern treatment, chronic invalidism or long hospitalization can still be the final outcome. These are the patients *par excellence* who 'know their own unconscious'. They lose their ego-boundary, having, as it were, dissolved their personalities out into the world of other people and outside objects; outside things also come back into them. This loss of identity can be a kind of death of the personality. We will try to make clearer, in later chapters, this confusion between inner and outer worlds.

There are six main symptoms in schizophrenia. These are generally accepted to be disorders of *thinking*, of the *emotions*, of the *will*, interference with the rate or coordination of *body movements* (catatonic symptoms), and the presence of *delusions* and *hallucinations*. Not all six symptoms need be present; any one may be absent, yet the diagnosis can still be schizophrenia. The symptoms are often so strange that one can say that the diagnosis of schizophrenia is to be made on the basis of their very 'non-understandability'. It has even been said that 'the form and content of the symptoms cannot be understood as arising emotionally, or rationally from the feeling state, the previous personality or the current situation of the patient.'[6] This extreme is not a view I subscribe to, or this book would have had a different title. We are mainly concerned at the moment, however, with description rather than understanding.

Disturbances in *thinking* can extend from a mild woolliness of thought to a private, non-communicating language. Here is part of something written by a patient to put in a patients' magazine I was editing:

> The mightiest hand of God is always down upon us,
> My own small tongue is just a tiny soul in size,
> It's cruel to understand the reason of God's power,
> That's why our hope is prouder by aboding earthened skies.
>
> His nightly drowning of our openness is hard to carry,
> By just a big onslaught which all our hearts adread,
> Good warmth with love we look for to acheer us,
> So upon the earthened skies it's homely born and fed.

It seemed precious to him and I published it as a poem. Some lines, indeed, have an almost poetic, although baffling quality.

A disturbance in thinking is a particularly important feature of schizophrenia and it has been said that all schizophrenics show a *formal thought disorder* if their illness lasts long enough. There have been many attempts to account for this symptom. These include the theory that there is an absence of central determining ideas, so that sequences of thought are determined by mere associations of sound, by alliteration, or unimportant details, and a false, synthetic series of concepts are created by a misuse of symbolization. That is to say, ideas are no longer ordered logically and abstractly but tend to become concrete, and may also merge together senselessly.

This 'autism', or 'phantasy thinking', has been further

analysed. The merging together of logically unrelated ideas has been called the *interpenetration of themes*, or *condensation*. Another feature is *over-inclusion*. This refers to the patient's problem in separating the relevant from the irrelevant. A psychotic adolescent boy, for example, when asked how long he had been at his school, spoke for twenty minutes, during which he not only ran back in time, but forward to what he would do on leaving school; in particular, he began reciting the A B C, and kept switching to counting in numbers. Time, letters, numbers, all quite different categories, were felt by him as equivalent to one another. He could not keep his thinking directed towards one goal, or generalizations and classes of things apart, but included different series of thoughts in his stream of consciousness.

Gestalt psychologists have used their principles both to try to describe and to explain schizophrenic thinking, just as earlier workers used association psychology. Thus Goldstein* developed a way of describing thinking in terms of *concrete* and *abstract attitudes*. In normal thinking an abstract attitude enables us to see objects as examples merely of one class or category, or another, and we can neglect unique aspects of an object in order to deal with it abstractly. This enables us to switch flexibly from one aspect of an object or situation to another, relate it to other abstractions and so on. A concrete attitude, however, implies an inability to generalize about the object; the object is seen with an immediate uniqueness; it claims all attention for that moment. Abstract thinking enables us to think ahead, to hypothesize, to manipulate our verbal and other symbols which stand in a generalized way for reality; we can also move back into ourselves for a moment, 'take thought', and move out again into the real

---

*Gestalt (configuration, pattern, form) psychology began both as a study of perception and as a brilliant, experimentally based reaction against earlier 'atomistic' psychologies. These latter had over-concerned themselves with the so-called raw elements of sensory experience. Gestalt psychology showed how this approach seriously neglected the unique wholeness and immediate self-organization of our perceptual experience – that a perceived whole is more than the mere sum of its perceived parts, just as hearing a tune, for example, is more than hearing a mere succession of notes. The Gestalt school went on from perceptual studies to apply their 'principles of organization' to learning, memory, social psychology, thinking, etc. Goldstein was one of these later workers.[7]

world. The schizophrenic is, however, 'stimulus-bound', and *even words themselves achieve a concreteness*, becoming 'things' in their own right, rather than existing as mere symbols which can stand in the place, often, of many slightly different things. Words, then, can hurt like blows, threaten like fists, dazzle, or bewilder with ambiguity like some half-remembered foreign saying.

Goldstein made the interesting suggestion that the fault in schizophrenia lies in the *isolation* of parts of the nervous system from one another. While this is unproven 'brain mythology', it is a way of trying to explain why patients respond so rigidly to events: only parts of them, in fact, respond. It has been suggested that this 'isolation' underlies the disorganization of the so-called 'figure-ground effect'. In normal conceptual thinking, important features of a situation stand out as a 'figure', against the 'ground' of the irrelevant. Lacking the ability to abstract the one from the other, the schizophrenic lacks concentration and cannot adapt himself from one situation to another. This lack of a figure-ground effect is also connected with the loss of the ego-boundary; the self-concept cannot be felt as a 'figure', demarcated and set apart from the inner and outer environments; the essential and the non-essential, the relevant and the irrelevant, all have equal importance. While we may ignore, here, Goldstein's references to neurology (he was also interested in illnesses where recognizable brain damage has been suffered), it is a fact that psychological tests show schizophrenics to be slower mentally than normal people. It has been pointed out that Goldstein's concept of 'concrete thinking' is probably concerned with the same thing described by the term 'over-inclusion'. Such changes in thinking would obviously produce a slowing-down in effective mental speed.

There has been a great deal of research into the thought disorder of schizophrenics and much of this work has been done by psychologists as well as psychiatrists; such a feature lends itself to testing. It is interesting to note that some of this work suggests the presence of 'some process' of variable intensity interfering with the patient's thoughts, which may not be just the 'hearing of voices'.

It is important to recognize that while thinking can be so changed, the *level of consciousness is not*. These patients are dreaming, as it were, wide awake. We all have curious states when we are just going to sleep or just waking which are vivid and dream-like – but we are not fully awake as schizophrenics are.

The stream of thought can itself become disordered. In *thought blocking* a gap appears in a sequence of thought, so that if the patient has been speaking he abruptly pauses, and when he speaks again he is off at a tangent, like a tape-recording with a piece arbitrarily cut out. Thought blocking of this kind may be responsible for the curious, aptly described 'knight's move in thought'. The patient will say, if asked, that thought blocking is unpleasant. Other patients may experience *pressure of thought*, when ideas seem to pour through their heads. Still others seem to have the opposite problem, that is, an apparent poverty of ideas. A thought disorder is often associated with a variety of curious ways of speaking, as could be expected. A fairly common one, common enough to be named, is *talking-past-the-point*, which is a clumsy translation from the German word *vorbeireden*. Here the patient talks somewhat, but not completely, irrelevantly. It has been noticed that this is not due to his misunderstanding us; in some cases it seems to arise from a 'playful' – not to say fatuous – attitude; in others, it may be a tactic to avoid contact with other people.[6]

The subjects that occupy a schizophrenic's thoughts are often very abstract – philosophy, spiritualism, religion, or power, for instance. The 'explanation may be no more than that through the medium of his illness the schizophrenic is confronted with the basic first questions of life.'[8] At any rate, the 'frequent close interest in religious, philosophical and mystical subjects . . . are issues of particular interest to the Christian community. Among candidates offering themselves for the religious vocation, there is invariably a percentage who, in the course of time, will develop schizophrenia . . .'[9] Yet, informed by genius, symptoms can contribute to the works of art of a Strindberg, a Van Gogh, or a Hölderlin.

The *emotional* changes in schizophrenia are also far-reaching; we only divide up the characteristics of a person into aspects, of course, for convenience of description; the thought changes we have already described inevitably have their impact on the total personality. Yet the emotions also alter, as it were, in their own right. A father may complain that he has lost all feeling for his family. He is puzzled and dismayed by this, and is aware of his loss. When this kind of feeling is a prominent symptom, it may amount to *depersonalization*. The patient knows that he is no longer 'locked on' to the environment by a repertoire of normal emotional responses. He feels he is now no longer himself. In so far as feelings are at the heart of ourselves, he feels he is no longer a person. This state may be accompanied by another, when the outside world seems to have altered, to have become alien – and unreal. This is called *derealization*. Depersonalization is not specific to schizophrenia. Sensitive, introverted individuals can experience it when depressed, and it appears in other syndromes too. Yet it is common in acute schizophrenia, often going on into manifest delusional states.

Young people, especially intelligent ones, developing schizophrenia, may become depressed as a reaction to their unnerving symptoms. Severe depressive illnesses are very uncommon in teenagers; a depression in this age group is much more likely to be the forerunner of a schizophrenic illness. The fear of madness itself can add to the distresses already multiplying and some young patients will respond to their new inner experiences with intense anxiety. They will seem to us both perplexed and afraid. Other patients, convinced that they have had super-human experiences, will strike us as ecstatic. Such a patient may describe feelings of exaltation, but we feel no rapport with him at all as he tells us he is Christ, or talks of his direct encounters with God. His transfiguration is our dismay.

In the chronic patient, the commonest emotional change, however, is emotional blunting. The capacity to experience appropriate emotions in any depth is gradually lost. Interestingly enough, the loss moves back regressively from the more tender, social feelings, those which should be aroused by family or friends, until even the primitive emotions – fear, hate and humour – become impoverished. Eroticism may survive, appearing ugly when the rest has faded. Schizophrenics, however, can sometimes show swift changes in feelings, from transient ecstasy to dread or despair. This may contribute to an act of violence towards the self or another. A striking feature of their emotionality is that it can be quite *incongruous*. It is, at such times, as though their feelings referred to a different time scale from their thoughts, or from the situation they find themselves in. Bad news may be greeted by fatuous giggling.

What of the disturbances of the *will*? To say 'the will', is really to say what a person does or does not do. A schizophrenic often complains, nevertheless, of weakening will-power. He thinks his thoughts and feelings, the words he uses and his behaviour, have all been imposed on him from outside and are beyond his control; he may feel impelled to keep doing the opposite of what is asked of him, or he may show *ambivalence*. This key term in psychiatry means an emotional attitude expressing simultaneously love and hate. For instance, ambivalence was neatly expressed when, in saying good-bye, a patient offered his clenched fist to shake.

Disturbances may be seen in the physical awkwardness and curious posture of some patients, as though they were expressing their inner state of feelings in mime. These symptoms can range from *stupor* to a chaotic *excitement*.

Of all the symptoms of madness *delusions* and *hallucinations* come first to mind. These are very characteristic symptoms of schizophrenia. A delusion is not easy to define without consigning all human beliefs to the realm of fairyland. Let us say that a delusion is 'a belief which is not true to fact, cannot be corrected by an appeal to the reason of the person entertaining it, and is out of harmony with the person's education and surroundings'.[10]

Some delusions are merely secondary, in the sense that the patient is trying to make sense of his strange experiences. He is rationalizing, as it were, the irrational. However, *primary* delusions are abnormal beliefs, very characteristic of this psychosis. They appear suddenly, carrying a ready-made and vivid sense of conviction.

A nurse from a famous teaching hospital suddenly believed that everyone thought she was a prostitute. At once the significance of ordinary objects changed. She began to have *ideas of reference*, that is, ideas that things in the outside world had special meanings for her. She saw a piece of newspaper blowing across an area of waste ground and was convinced that it was full of vile stories about her. She knew this, even though she had not read the paper.

A delusion can arise out of an unusual *delusional mood*, one in which the patient feels that the significance of his life situation is changing in some uncanny way – that his environment has become threatening, or that he is understanding it for the first time. The experience may be a frightening, bewildering, or joyous one; out of the mood emerges like a light out of darkness a new, unquestioned, compelling belief; a delusion that he is a King, or that she is a tart, or that the Jews are plotting against the world. The contents of delusions are influenced by the patients' social milieu. The most common sorts in schizophrenia are those of persecution; there can, however, be delusions of grandeur, or more commonly, of hypochondriasis, the latter being quite bizarre, with weird sensations in the body and ideas of physical malfunctioning of an impossible kind. A patient may believe, for example, that his brain is being burned by electricity, or that he is being 'tortured sexually'. This is hypochondriasis of an entirely different order from the neurotic sort. *Paranoid*, or persecutory delusions are often as bizarre; a patient may believe, for example, that she is being sexually interfered with from a distance, either by some known agency – Communists, or whatever – or perhaps by some kind of contemporary technology, such as radar or television. Delusional experience frequently goes with hallucinations, the false belief augmenting the false perception, or the hallucination giving confirmation to the patient's unreal belief.

Hallucinations are 'mental impressions of sensory vividness, occurring without external stimulus'.[10] Auditory hallucinations are the most characteristic, as schizophrenics often 'hear voices'. However, other experiences, such as hallucinations of touch, smell, or taste, or odd feelings in the body, often in the genitals, may exist too. These voices may be abusive, even obscene; the psychotic patient may answer the voices, returning abuse for abuse. This tendency to reply can be very upsetting to the uninformed witness – a relation or bystander. It is easy to see why primitive peoples should think that a person complaining of voices in his head, or coming from different parts of his body, is 'possessed'. Indeed, the patient himself may believe this and say so, even in our society. Since we do not believe in possession, it is hard to explain the phenomenon. One suggestion has been that hallucinations are a product of dissociation – a part of the patient's mind, which has been separated off, reappears as a hallucinatory voice, being 'referred' unconsciously to different parts of his body or out into the world. The voices are most commonly persecutory, as are delusions. They are also often concerned with sexual themes – referring to homosexuality, intercourse, or masturbation in unpleasant, accusatory ways.

The attitudes of patients to their experience varies. Chronic patients may be indifferent to their 'voices'; patients newly ill may be very distressed. Some may claim that radio or atomic radiations, or spirits of one kind or another are behind the voices. Others are bewildered and depressed. Even if the voices don't urge them to kill themselves, as they may, a few are depressed enough to commit suicide because of the horror that can attend the disintegration of the self.

*

As we have said, any or all of the six main symptoms of schizophrenia – disturbances of thinking, the emotions, the will, interference with body movements, delusions and hallucinations – may be present. Perhaps it is now a little clearer why psychiatrists need special descriptive terms, and find classifications difficult.

There are many ways of describing different forms of schizophrenia.[6] A simple one is still the widest used.[8,10] This consists of four groupings: *simple*, *hebephrenic*, *catatonic* and *paranoid*.

1. *Simple schizophrenia* starts around adolescence, or a little later. *Shallowness of emotionality* is the principal symptom, with indifference amounting sometimes to callousness, and an increasing lack of drive. The course is usually insidious. As the personality is eroded away over the years, the patient is often unable to keep up with his job. He drifts down in society, into poverty, social isolation and sometimes crime or vagrancy.

2. *Hebephrenic schizophrenia* starts a little later. Again, the development is usually insidious. In addition to a shallow affect, *one or another of the forms of thought disorder* appears. Delusions and hallucinations gradually emerge, and they may be phantastic. Neurotic, hypochondriacal behaviour can at first mask the true, basically psychotic process. A brilliant schoolboy may start falling off in performance, failing exams as he becomes less and less able to concentrate. He may end up in a permanently dreamy state, or fatuous and silly. Persons between puberty and the middle twenties are the chief victims. Hebephrenics are often preoccupied

with the basic questions of life and the vaster problems of philosophy or science, while they themselves become increasingly unable to cope with day-to-day living, affecting strange *mannerisms* and perplexed by odd experiences.

Depression in a young person may be the first early sign of hebephrenia, obsessionality also. *Depersonalization*, loss of the sense of existing as a person, and *derealization*, feeling the outside world is unreal, are other possible early symptoms. Suicidal attempts may be made; behaviour becomes peculiar and childish.

3. *Catatonic schizophrenia* starts in the late teens or early twenties. It may begin after a period of insomnia and depression, with increasing withdrawal from contact with the environment. In this illness there may be strange grimacing and twitching of the facial muscles. A refusal to comply with requests may be accompanied by hallucinations and delusions. A catatonic patient in this phase may be mute, refusing food or attention; he may repeat some phrase constantly.

Stupor is the commonest initial symptom of catatonia. In stupor the patient seems completely *withdrawn* and inaccessible. He takes up strange bodily attitudes and may be completely immobilized physically, or merely pass through phases of being unable to make some few movements. His *posturing* can be obviously symbolic, as when he holds his arms out for hours as though crucified; or he may stand awkwardly immobile in some other way. He often refuses to comply with requests and takes on weird mannerisms.

Interestingly enough, despite having been 'lost' in a catatonic stupor, a patient when he recovers often gives an accurate account of everything that happened to him: which person was unkind to him, who was helpful. Thus memory and perception remain intact, despite an apparent annihilation of the whole personality. Environment continues to be important. As Freud put it, 'even in conditions so far removed from the reality of the external world as hallucinatory confusional states, one learns from patients after their recovery that at the time in some corner of their minds, as they express it, there was a normal person hidden, who watched the hubbub of the illness go past, like a disinterested spectator.'[11]

In catatonic states there can also be sudden outbursts of

agitation; catatonic schizophrenia may start as an abrupt explosion of psychotic excitement. This is as incoherent as the patient's thinking. His internal experiences are so distorted by his thought disorder, and his emotions by his hallucinations and delusions, that he may need to invent new words, *neologisms*, to try to communicate the bizarre uniqueness of his inner world. In any case, an excited catatonic schizophrenic is likely to have a speech disorder, his speech being incoherent, a *word-salad*. This contrasts with the *flight of ideas* that an acutely manic patient shows: a stream of associations, which may be witty, punning or linked by the mere sound of the words. A flight of ideas has some easily discernible structure, however. A word-salad has not. The catatonic may invent a secret language. In his excitement he is absurd, impulsive and 'fragmented'.

4. *Paranoid schizophrenia*, the last group, comes on later in life than the others, usually in the thirties. Primary delusions, followed by secondary 'delusional interpretations' (rationalizations) and hallucinations make up the main features. The personality may otherwise be relatively preserved for a long time. The delusions are those of persecution – ideas of being watched, followed, talked about, plotted against; the 'voices' are hostile and reviling. There can be considerable variation in the amount of disturbance, as one person may keep his strange knowledge that he is being tortured by hypnosis or electricity to himself, while another feels so persecuted that he becomes disabled. Delusions may be grandiose as well as persecutory. *Paraphrenia* and *paranoia* are sub-groups of paranoid schizophrenia which were thought to have special characteristics. There does not seem much point in separating these groups. If they are followed up long enough, symptoms emerge that join them to the general group already outlined.

*

The earlier and more insidious forms of schizophrenia are usually much more destructive than the acute attacks of the illnesses of later onset, as though the more mature personality of the older person could resist disintegration more effectively. Schizophrenia may be remittent, but, contrary to depressive illnesses, attacks can leave great residual damage to the personality. The importance of this lies not only, of course, in its implications for the patient, but also for the community. This remittent course accounts for the existence of a population of 'chronic' schizophrenics. It may be easy to label many patients as 'schizophrenic', but with others, despite or because of the broad definition of this illness, diagnosis can be very difficult. Even well-trained psychiatrists use different criteria for making their diagnoses.[12] However, although there are doubts over diagnosis, an approximate prognosis can still be made. About one-quarter of schizophrenics eventually show severe deterioration of personality. About another quarter are left with less severe defects. The third quarter show only a slight defect, and the rest recover from their attack.

Schizophrenic Syndrome in Children[13] – Childhood Psychosis[14] – Early Infantile Autism.[15]

Even a child can be psychotic.

George was three-and-a-half years old. He had always lived in a crowded, residential nursery and had never seen his parents. We know that this in itself can be desperately damaging, but something else had happened, producing a different condition from that resulting simply from deprivation.

A strikingly handsome little boy, he sat on the floor of the nursery, apart from and oblivious to the rest of the children who were running about. At first he gave the impression of being mentally backward; yet he was successfully spinning wooden blocks round and round, as he had done for a long time now. He had rather a fixed, vacant grin, directed to his playthings and not to any person. He made no effort to adjust physically when being picked up, neither raising his arms nor moulding his body to the person carrying him. He gave you a curious feeling that you did not exist. He was mute as he played with the doctor's hand, playing with it as though it were a toy, as though it ended at the wrist. He seemed only to perceive the hand. The hand was an object.

While schizophrenia of the adult type can begin, very rarely, in later childhood, serious mental illness of this type can also be found in very early childhood, and it is sufficiently different from the adult condition to warrant a separate name. Some children suffering from this illness have abnormal brain waves and have been found to have abnormal brain metabolism. The rest, however, show no discernible physical defects sufficient to account for their illness.

Although the condition is rare, it seems worth while describing, if only because until recently educational and medical facilities for these children were so poor that their parents had to form a society to press for improvement,* a curious comment on the 'Welfare State'. The parents of any child with a handicap may obviously need special help with their child, if it only amounts to dealing with the severe guilt that they so often feel at having a handicapped child. The commonest phantasy of a woman is that her child might be deformed. Her first question at the end of labour is 'Is the baby all right?'

A psychotic child fails to relate emotionally in a proper fashion, or at all, to other people. He seems unaware of his own identity, sometimes repeatedly examining some part of his body, as though it did not belong to him. Such a child may only play with one object in a fixed way, a way perhaps quite odd. In some cases he seems to strive to keep everything around him – furniture, toys – exactly the same. Reactions to pain, or to things seen or heard, are sometimes abnormal. George, for example, could fall over quite hard and not cry.

There may be episodes of acute anxiety, difficult or impossible for his parents to understand. Speech may never be acquired, or may be lost. The general behaviour of the child is unusual, his activity being greater or much less than in a normal child. He may exhibit bizarre postures, or show curious mannerisms and carry out repeated rituals of an apparently meaningless kind. The prognosis is generally worse when speech has not been achieved or regained by five years of age.

It is important to distinguish between the autistic child and the one who is mentally retarded, because they require quite different handling. As in the case of adult schizophrenia, the total picture varies according to the particular individual. The impairment of emotional relationships is the commonest feature in a child showing serious mental retardation, with patches of almost normal or even superior ability. He thus differs from the child who is simply mentally subnormal, for such a child is globally retarded, slow in everything, yet still relates emotionally to others.

*The Society for Autistic Children.

The Puerperal Psychoses

It seems logical to mention this group of illnesses here, between those just described, where on the whole physical causes are very rare, yet to be determined, or only contributory, and the next group, where physical factors are essential causes. This is because the psychotic episodes that may arise in the puerperium – the period following childbirth – follow a very physical form of stress (labour is well named). In fact, these illnesses seem to have no very special character of their own and childbirth, a deeply moving emotional event as well as a physical test, is sometimes followed by a schizophrenic illness or, more commonly, an affective illness,[16] almost indistinguishable from those we have described already. It is, however, worth while noting the generalization that whenever a particular environmental or physical event stands out as an important precipitating factor the prognosis is more favourable than where a psychosis arises without apparent cause. The disturbance of the relationship between a psychotic mother and her new baby has obvious social implications, as well as medical ones. The control of puerperal infections has greatly reduced the incidence of this mental illness.

Organic Psychoses – Organic Disorders – Deliria

This group contrasts with all the previous mental illnesses we have considered in that we can classify by causes in the traditional, medical way. The conditions are clearly produced by physical influences on the brain, or by damage to the brain itself. Physical disease, injury, or the effects of the physical changes of ageing, can produce a major mental disorder.

Over and above the basic symptoms, which are fairly uniform, an individual colouring of symptoms will always be present. This reflects the previous personality and experiences of the person affected. The patient remains unique, even if he can be classified. His uniqueness may often, alas, be expressed by an exaggeration of previous personality traits. The thrifty become miserly; the rather serious person, openly depressed.

An organic psychosis can be either an acute or a chronic illness. When acute, it is usually the result of some toxic process affecting the brain. This kind of psychosis has been called 'symptomatic' and is usually potentially reversible. The delirium of an acute fever is an example of this. The mental symptoms are just part of the symptoms of the fever. The patient is in an *acute confusional state* or *delirium*.

On the other hand chronic mental illnesses can arise when fairly severe brain damage has occurred. Syphilis, which affects the central nervous system is one, now comparatively rare; *senile dementia* (second childhood) is another. Brain tissue, once damaged, cannot repair itself, except by forming scars; hence the chronicity. The patient is in a *chronic confusional state*, (*chronic delirium*).

The fragile old lady sat on the edge of her bed in the ward, smiling and chatting away. Her clothes were in disarray but she did not seem to notice this. She could not remember what she had had for lunch, though she had greedily eaten it only ten minutes before. She was insisting that she was twenty-five years old (she was seventy-five), when, abruptly, she began to cry, angrily, for no obvious reason.

We can generalize fairly accurately about the symptoms of the whole group of organic mental disorders. *Intelligence* is affected; *understanding* and *memory* deteriorate and the past is more real than the present. The patient's *sense of time and place is disorientated*, and his level of *concentration* alters from minute to minute. Like a small child, he cannot pay *attention* for long. The emotions become unstable and changeable, with abrupt swings from pointless euphoria to equally inappropriate anger or weeping (a so-called *labile affect*). Behaviour coarsens and character becomes less worthy than before, or more childish, or both. One set of symptoms may stand out more than another in any particular case.

In the acute cases, usually secondary to some general physical illness, delirium – which is made up of *disorientation* and *hallucinations*, together with loss of memory of recent events – is the commonest form of the psychosis.

*

We should emphasize, in passing, the theoretical interest of 'organic psychoses' caused by drugs. Many substances can affect the brain and produce mental disorder.[17] Great interest has been shown in one group, the 'hallucinogens'. Mescaline, for example, a preparation of cactus, was probably known to the Aztecs, and has had a distinct vogue in recent years, both amongst psychiatrists seeking new treatment for their patients, and intellectuals looking for new experiences. The effects are largely visual, and visual images can take the place of thinking and feeling and mood, as in a dream. Time can become slowed down, or existence timeless. Sensations may be strangely crosslinked, so that sounds produce visual effects. Depersonalization often occurs after intoxication with this drug, as does derealization. Lysergic acid diethylamide (L.S.D.), a drug of even greater potency, has become the most widely known of the hallucinogens. On the one hand these drugs have been called sacred, and their ability to 'expand consciousness' has been seen as a possibility of transcendental experience, to be treated with religious or mystical reverence. On the other, many unpleasant or even dangerous effects have been described in the casual or incompetent use of the drugs, including murder, suicide and the precipitation of true psychotic states. Sometimes a 'trip', as the drug experience has been called, can recur spontaneously days or months later (*British Medical Journal*, 1966, vol. 1, p. 1945). It is hard not to believe, nevertheless, that under expert guidance, some individuals might find value in going through altered states of consciousness in response to these substances. (cf. R. D. Laing, *The Politics of Experience* and *The Bird of Paradise*, Penguin, 1966.)

Since a drug in extremely small quantities can cause such psychotic-like symptoms, *one should always remember that there may be physical factors contributing to the functional psychoses*, schizophrenia, or manic depressive psychosis that are yet unknown. There is, for example, a condition, *recurrent catatonia*, in which abnormal metabolism is to blame. Described by Gjessing in 1939, it yields to rational treatment by diet and drugs. However, recurrent catatonia is very rare, and the hallucinogens produce more often the picture of toxic deliria than of schizophrenia. In the present state of knowledge, emotional and social factors alone can be shown to account for a great deal.

In this chapter we have been imposing names on clusters of symptoms shown by sick people. This will enable us to talk about these people more easily and thus come to a better understanding of them. Let us turn now to cultural factors.

Cultural Influences

There is now massive evidence that different cultures – the way of life of each society – tend to produce different personalities. Each society has a particular vision of maleness, of femaleness, of rights and obligations. There are different kinds of status and different roles for each member of one society, compared with those of another. There are different ways of bringing up children so that they will become integrated into their culture, and will express it by the way they live.[1-7] The total education of children from their earliest days is in one mould rather than another. The thinking of children, their ideas, their consciences, their attitudes towards the supernatural, and all the rest, are imposed upon them by the society which intimately surrounds them as they grow up. We can think of a basic personality structure – a personality which best fits into the range of institutions, roles and habits of a particular culture – even allowing for special acceptable, individual variations, by referring to these variations as character.[1] An individual having acquired such a 'basic personality' will be thought of as 'normal' in his society. Yet he may seem very odd to us.

I wish to touch on cultural factors only to see what light they can throw on psychosis. One of the motives behind various studies of cultures has been to see if one kind or another could afford protection against mental disorder. The fact that the incidence and prevalence of the different disorders varies in different cultures certainly requires explanation. There is, however, no society in which mental illness is unknown or unrecognized in one form or another.

Normality can be very different in different societies. These

differences account to a large extent for the reported variations in
the incidence of mental abnormalities in these societies. How far
does our own stereotyped vision of a masculine man, or a
feminine woman reach? The ideal *Arapesh* male is gentle and
responsive. The Arapesh expect and find that their women have
similar personalities. Their child care is mild and cooperative,
without aggression. Their children are never punished. For the
Arapesh, aggression is shocking, unpleasant, bad form. En-
terprise, self-assertion, competitiveness (things near the heart of
our own culture) receive profound social disapproval. Anger is
shocking. The *Zuni* Indians resemble the Arapesh in abhorring
assertiveness: their leaders have to be forced into the role and are
then treated with disrespect. Yet violent and aggressive men and
women are the normal people of the *Mundugumor*. Their pattern
of child care is severe, aggressive, without mutual aid. Their
cultural assumption is of a basic hostility between members of
the same sex. Their way of bringing up their children ensures that
their hypothesis is borne out in adult behaviour. There is even a
society where male and female roles are more or less reversed.
With the *Tchambuli*, it is the male who is emotionally dependent
and thought to be less responsible, while the female is managing,
dominant and impersonal.

Primitive peoples reject some individuals just as we do. We
reject, for example, prostitutes or delinquents, homosexuals or
the mentally disordered. However, they do not always reject the
same type of person, for social rejection reflects the norms of the
society in question. Thus, aggressive people tend to be rejected
by us and even more emphatically by the Zuni or the Arapesh.
Kind, generous people, thought to be normal in our culture, would
be thought very odd among the Mundugumor or the *Dobuan*.

When it comes to psychotic symptoms, we find that cultures
vary widely in accepting or rejecting an individual showing the
'symptom'. Some symptoms may not be seen as abnormalities
at all. Ideas of persecution are reasonable in Dobu. They fit into
the Dobuan system of relationships. Grandiose ideas are not
paranoid and unreal for the *Kwakiutl* Indian, but, equally sensibly, fit into his vigorous life, where ostentatious display and
extravagance to impress others is the mainspring of society. Even
hallucinations, so often thought typical of madness, do not lead

to social rejection among the *Mohave* or *Takala*: '... there are societies in which cataleptic seizures are marks of nobility or in which paranoid behaviour is virtuous ... within his everyday behaviour the Yurok cries to his gods like a baby; he hallucinates in his meditations like a psychotic...'[7]

Yet the examination of cultures very foreign to our own does not reveal mere formal sets of customs blindly carried out. Rather, one discovers human beings living social lives which are based on assumptions entirely different from our own. Furthermore the patterns of social behaviour which arise from these assumptions make sense in their own terms. They are mutually consistent, and fit in logically with the ideas behind them. Familiarity with a particular primitive culture can show, as our few short examples suggested, why a personality feature we call abnormal could be thought normal elsewhere. Kimball Young, writing of the 'norm' in Bali, comments on *the parallels to be found among our schizophrenic patients*, adding, 'we must not forget that the common acceptances and expectancies – which in Bali are put chiefly into group ceremonials – provide a standard of conformity and interaction that is, for the self and others, normal and proper.'[8]

The major point is then that the symptoms of psychosis are *relative to our culture*. Perhaps an 'absolute' psychosis does exist, but we seem to have only social criteria to detect symptoms. In this sense, all symptoms are relative to the culture in which they appear.

It could be argued that acute mania, extreme depression, chaotic confusional states, or withdrawal to the point of loss of contact, are all thought abnormal anywhere. Yet this does not seem to be true. A society somewhere sees one or other state as holy or curative, even if elsewhere it seems an illness – or the result of a curse.

If we accept that normality and deviations from normality can only be culturally defined, we are left in a quandary, as though our medical concept of psychosis had been destroyed by relativity; we must accept that each society is unique and that its 'norms' have a statistical basis peculiar to its culture. 'Abnorms', therefore – what is held to be abnormal in thought, speech or act – depend on these variable definitions of normality.

It seems to me that the right way out of this maze is to grasp that *'what has clearly emerged from studies of the incidence of mental disorder under different cultural conditions is that the threshold of public tolerance towards mental illness varies greatly, and it is this variation that may be responsible for apparent differences of incidence'*.[9] Halmos goes further than this: 'In rejecting cultural relativism, I have insisted that abnormality is not a thing that varies according to culture, but that cultures vary *according to the degree of abnormality they encourage and legitimize.'*[10] He goes on to argue powerfully that while 'normality' may be indefinable in any way true for all cultures (just as in general medicine, doctors find defining 'health' very difficult), there is already substantial agreement as to what amounts to mental abnormality. Thus, he says, the *description* of a paranoid syndrome would be basically the same given by any one psychiatrist of any orientation, even if his language, conceptual schemes and assumptions were to differ substantially from another's.

It is worth lingering on these important ideas, because they will justify the approach to understanding psychosis that we are going to take in the next few chapters. Halmos recognizes and acknowledges the difficulties in thinking clearly about normality and abnormality, and also sees how these two concepts are linked one to another. He dismisses the terms 'adjustment' as a measure of mental health, seeking a less superficial or 'culture-bound' definition. He quotes Frank's definition of adjustment (which is a fairly typical one): 'The ancient dichotomy of the individual and society will sooner or later be resolved as we understand that society is in each individual, and what we call "social adjustment" is essentially the individual's relation to himself.' Halmos points out that 'adjustment' is a psychodynamic compromise. A psychotic could be 'adjusted' within the meaning of many common definitions of the word, as he quietly hallucinates away.

It follows, then, that some attempt should be made to describe an *absolute* norm and an *absolute* abnorm, of a kind common to all humanity. Halmos claims that 'the bio-psychological potentialities, i.e. inherited potentialities of human beings, are not realized in the majority behaviour of any culture.'

He also claims that these potentialities constitute the 'ontological basis of the pan-human norm'. He admits that this norm is always 'culturally contaminated', that it can never be observed pure, that it is only to be inferred. He rejects 'norm' as meaning 'desirable'; that is to say, as an evaluating term. He puts forward the argument that norms and abnorms arise out of the early experiences of childhood. In particular, he cites the mother-child relationship and the influences of child-raising practices in the first five years of life. He also stresses the importance of threats to the child or his 'love objects'. He believes that parental instability is relevant, and so is culturally determined 'teasing' of the child. His use of terms reminds us of the way Erik Erikson uses the words 'basic trust' and 'mistrust'.[7] When speaking of an infant's experience of his mother and the infant's 'first social achievement' when 'she has become an inner certainty, as well as an outer predictability', he says:

Such consistency, continuity and sameness of experience provide a rudimentary sense of ego identity which depends, I think, on the recognition that there is an inner population of remembered and anticipated sensations and images which are firmly correlated with the outer population of familiar and predictable things and people ... the absence of basic trust can best be studied in infantile schizophrenia, while life-long underlying weakness of such trust is apparent in adult personalities in whom withdrawal into schizoid and depressive states is habitual ... the bizarreness and withdrawal in the behaviour of many very sick individuals hides an attempt to recover social mutuality by a testing of the borderlines between senses and physical reality, between words and social meaning.

An assumption in our own text will be then that, as regards psychosis, abnormality is not anything that varies according to culture, but that, as Halmos says, cultures vary according to the degree of abnormality they encourage and legitimize. There are 'absolute psychoses'. In an earlier section we discussed the integrity of the personality in such terms as ego structure and ego strength. It follows that it would be possible to describe culture patterns in these terms, in terms of the degree of the culturally approved, ignored, or even discouraged command over raw instinctual forces present in typical individuals in the culture. Individuals in some cultures are more 'self-conscious' than those in others. And we would also trace back the origins of basic trust or mistrust (ontological security or insecurity) to the childhood

experiences of individuals in the culture, beginning with the
characteristic mother-child relationship each society prefers. In
this relationship are found the beginnings both of socialization
and of individual being. It follows that with the above views,
conformist individuals in abnormal cultures – such as the Yurok
or the Dobuan – are in fact abnormal in an absolute sense, even
though they find complete acceptance within their own culture.
The ultimate justification for these judgements is to be found in
the descriptive system chosen earlier to characterize mental life,
and which will be developed in rather more detail in later chapters. It is a descriptive system which permits 'more or less mature',
'more highly, or less highly evolved', 'more or less integrated'
to be ascribed to individuals or to societies in detailed psychological terms. Not all authors would agree with this viewpoint;
but in this text we are in fact rejecting the 'cultural relativity'
idea of symptoms with regard to psychoses.

The incidence and prevalence rates of psychotic illnesses are
related, therefore, to the social characteristics of a patient's
environment, to levels of social tolerance and intolerance. The
clearest connexion between the symptoms themselves and the
individual's life experiences has been established by the study of
schizophrenic delusions. Other symptoms, or forms of this illness,
can be linked to social forces with very much less certainty. Let
us now turn to Western cultures.

An American study found that American men formulated their
grandiose delusions in terms of wealth. Foreign-born men did so
more in terms of artistic or literary ability. The American negro
tended to be religiously deluded; and whereas white women were
more paranoid than white men, who were grandiose, negro
women reversed this feature. Paranoid ideas characterized the
delusions of negroes from the competitive northern states, and
also went with a poor educational background.[11] These are
features we can understand, in terms of *content*. We can think of a
materialistic culture, with very unevenly distributed privileges
producing these different features. We must distinguish content
from *cause*, however, and not go beyond this kind of evidence to say that the environment caused the person to be
deluded.

A more recent British study of schizophrenic delusions also

found interesting differences associated with different social factors.[12]

Grandiose delusions were more frequent in persons of higher social or educational status, and in the eldest rather than the youngest siblings. Delusions of inferiority had an opposite distribution. Paranoid delusions increased in frequency with increasing age, and were more common to immigrants in the areas studied than to those native to them. As with grandiose delusions, delusions of a religious or supernatural kind were more frequent in those of higher social status, and were commoner in the single than in the married. Sexual delusions were found much more often in women than in men, and were more common in the married, oddly enough, than in the single.

It is interesting to recall that masturbation was widely believed, a hundred years ago, to be a cause of insanity. Certainly, many psychotic patients masturbate openly and frequently, and we can see that such an association with insanity could be thought a causal one.[13] Such a sexually based hypothesis might seem shrewd for its time if we erroneously held sex to be the single explanatory principle for all mental health and disease. Yet a study of the records of the Bethlem Royal Hospital of a hundred years ago shows that the main content of delusions in mid-Victorian times was religious in character.[14] The authors of this study were attempting to establish whether the clinical picture of schizophrenia had altered through the years. They certainly found 'sexual preoccupations' in the patients of a hundred years ago, but to a much lesser degree than religious ones, and to a much lesser extent than in their current control group. As the authors commented, the mid-nineteenth century in England is considered a period of sexual repression. We could have expected outpourings of sexual material during acute schizophrenic illness. And yet twice as many twentieth-century schizophrenics had sexual preoccupations as did nineteenth-century schizophrenics. Here, very clearly, the main preoccupations of the time colour the contents of delusions.

A connexion does exist between the content of psychotic delusions and social factors, but the influence of those factors is much less clearly linked to other features of schizophrenia. This does not mean, however, that we cannot establish associations between environmental conditions and schizophrenia or other psychoses.

In considering environmental conditions, one must not forget the question of inheritance. Too often, otherwise brilliant studies of family psychodynamics* totally ignore the possibilities of inheritance, making it very hard to evaluate the picture of family life that emerges. We can well understand from the symptoms of psychosis we have described that great stresses can be caused by them in a family trying to support and contain the person so afflicted. The family problem has been graphically described by Enid Mills in her book *Living With Mental Illness*.[15] However, it can be very difficult to establish cause and effect in such a family; to decide how far a family is reacting to the stress imposed on it by its disturbed member or how far it is itself responsible for the latter's disturbance by its manner of communicating with him. If, in fact, the main cause of the psychotic behaviour is a heavy genetic loading, a psychodynamic study remains interesting, but it misses a major point.

In the 'nature versus nurture' problem the modern approach is not to oppose the two factors, but rather to view our constitutions as the result of a continual interaction between inheritance and environment.[16] Psychiatrists are now concerned with the relative importance of both. Thus an examination of the families of manic-depressive patients revealed that the risk of manic-depressive psychosis was higher if home conditions were poor.[17] The two factors interacted.

*

Environmental factors, and other important features associated with psychotic illness, are extremely difficult to measure. The effects of social isolation, broken homes, bereavement, maternal deprivation and social class all need to be precisely defined in their relationship to psychosis. As E. H. Hare says,[18] maternal deprivation could be assessed according to a physician's judgement

*By psychodynamic is meant the study of psychology from the point of view of the causative factors in mental activity, with particular attention to drives and motives. The approach is typical of psychoanalysis, where unconscious motivation is especially stressed. (An interesting suggestion that this is an exercise in semantics has been made; see C. Rycroft, (ed.), 'Psychoanalysis Observed', *Causes and Meaning*, Constable, 1966.)

of whether a person did or did not receive a reasonable degree of maternal love in early childhood – this is a subjective judgement; or it could be assessed in terms of physical separation. We are so suspicious of subjective judgements that the first sort of assessment would be thought to provide 'soft data', being unreliable; the second – 'hard data' – is more reliable and scientific, but it may be irrelevant to the concept we wish to represent and quantify.

Among other simple things to measure is the married versus single state. When many patients are examined, it is found that the seriously mentally disordered are far more often single than married. It is of course possible to argue from this that marriage protects an individual in some way from psychosis. This may be true sometimes. However, it seems more often the case that the personality problems that lead to psychosis explain also the singleness. That is to say, singleness is also an expression of the illness. This view is supported by the fact that there is a far higher rate of admission to mental hospitals of divorced people than of widowed people. In other words, both failure to marry and failure in marriage may be symptoms of the same basic disorder.

Looking at different parts of a particular country we find striking differences in the distribution of the mentally disordered. There are higher admission rates in towns than in the country. While some of these differences can be explained by the superior admission facilities in towns, an examination of the populations living in towns and a comparison of these with those living in the country has shown that the types of population differ, and this accounts to a very real extent for the different admission rates. It appears that there is a higher percentage of psychotics living in towns, whereas epileptics and the mentally subnormal are commoner in the country, where, perhaps, country life is more congenial for them.

However, a very intriguing feature of mental hospital admission rates is how much they vary in different parts of a city. This is particularly true of schizophrenia. The highest admission rates are to be found in the centres of cities.[19] The outer, usually newer and more prosperous parts of large towns have markedly lower rates. There are at least two possible explanations for this. The first is that older, dilapidated city centres are environments that contribute causally to schizophrenia. Alternatively it could be argued that these patients have come down into the poorer areas of a town because their symptoms lead to social inadequacy. Perhaps, also, they may have drifted there away from personal relationships that they could not handle elsewhere. The first study of schizophrenics in cities was in Chicago in 1939. This study has been repeated and now confirmed in many cities, including British ones. In the original study it was thought the explanation was that the social isolation of old city centres was itself a causal factor in schizophrenia. Certainly other similar studies show that high rates of schizophrenia are associated with 'single-person households': bedsitters, rooming houses and so on. Sheer population density does not seem to be a related factor, for all one's impressions of the 'pressure of numbers' in overcrowded slum areas.

Manic-depressive psychosis, however, finds its highest incidence in the more well-to-do districts.[19] It is often said that we are a class-ridden nation. How does class relate to psychosis? Class, or socio-economic status, must be defined in some way and this is usually done by occupation. There is a very different incidence of schizophrenia in one class as compared with another. In one study, the rate in the lowest social class was ten times that found in the highest. Other studies with less dramatic contrasts nevertheless clearly show the same pattern. What is the explanation for this difference in the types of psychosis between the locations and classes of people – is it simply that working-class people have schizophrenia, and middle-class people have affective disorders? (There is evidence that social class influences the diagnosis itself. That is, the doctor, usually a middle-class person, is biased. There seems to be a definite suggestion in some studies at any rate, that patients with *similar symptoms* may receive different diagnoses, depending on their particular social background, patients from the lower socio-economic groups being more often diagnosed schizophrenic than manic-depressive, higher social status patients receiving more often the label 'manic-depressive'. American findings suggest that class in America also influences the nature of the treatment provided.[20])

The real answer seems to emerge to a considerable extent from the differences between schizophrenia and manic-depressive illness. In discussing manic-depressive psychosis in the chapter on labels, we said that one of its cardinal features was that an attack left the personality unimpaired. A person might be ill for some weeks or months, but on recovery he could pick up the same threads of life as before. Attacks of schizophrenia are different. This disorder may be more chronic; the personality may become increasingly distorted and damaged; its recovery is often incomplete. The same features that lead to drifting down into areas of cheap, bad housing will lead to taking up badly paid jobs, unskilled labouring, working as sandwich-board men, or in kitchens, or not working at all. Therefore our method of 'classing' people by occupation alone is often a particularly deceptive criterion for schizophrenics, who tend to be socially mobile, often in a downward direction.

Does intelligence defend one against psychosis? Opinions vary up to a point. There is, however, a very impressive American survey on the subject, the Terman 'Gifted Group Study'.[21] In this a reasonably large number of exceptionally gifted children have been followed on into adulthood. That is to say, 1,500 children, few of whom have been lost track of, have been studied for over thirty-seven years and the experiment continues. Although not perfect as a psychiatric investigation, this study has produced the interesting finding that so far, at any rate, the 'Gifted Group' does not differ greatly from the general population. It has been just as liable to mental illness.

The influence of religion and the structural compactness of a community have also been investigated, with the expectation that these factors might be more conducive to mental health. A well-known example of such research is the one in which the Hutterite community in North America was examined to see if it was more resistant than other societies to mental illness because of being a more coherent, socially organized community, based on agricultural settlements. The hypothesis was proved wrong, for there was found to be a fairly large amount of psychosis in this population. Nevertheless, the type of psychosis contrasted with that of neighbouring populations with different traditions. This particular example is one we will return to in discussing a 'guilt culture', and the relationship of guilt to depressive illness. The Hutterites have much depressive illness in their community.

Cultures which use 'shaming' methods to control the behaviour of individuals rather than our 'inner conscience' method have low depression rates (and suicide is almost non-existent).

The United Kingdom has only very recently acquired a large immigrant population. Much of our data on immigrants comes from American and other studies which have the advantage of showing changes over more than one generation. Migrants do seem to have a higher incidence of psychosis than either their native populations or their adopted ones, which has been interpreted as indicating that the urge to migrate can itself arise from emotional instability. This view, I think, fails to allow sufficiently for the impact of one culture upon another. In fact, other work shows that psychosis rates are higher among recent immigrants than among earlier ones, who have had time to grow accustomed to new ways. Presumably the truth lies sometimes with one view, sometimes with another; in other cases both factors may combine. That is to say, sometimes an incipient psychosis lies behind the urge to emigrate; sometimes the act of emigrating and of changing environment makes radical demands in terms of adaptation which are beyond a person's capacity; sometimes both circumstances operate together. In contrast to these facts about migration from one country to another, migration within a country may be an expression of greater constitutional toughness, the result of seeking better opportunities and of showing initiative. Fewer of these migrants are emotionally disturbed than the average for the country.[22] This is an important fact to know when, in our second industrial revolution with old industries closing down and new ones opening up elsewhere, the mobility of our labour force is becoming more and more important.

*

What really constitutes a 'case'? We began this chapter by attempting to make clear that a case is defined in each society by its own criteria. In our own culture, why does a person go to a doctor about his nerves, or to complain about a relative? He does not talk about his symptoms in psychiatric jargon. Re-admission to mental hospitals more often follows a social crisis of one kind or another than an increase in psychiatric symptoms, and it is of this crisis that the patient or his family may complain.

Thus in a study of a group of discharged schizophrenics, while there was clinical deterioration (delusions were the prominent clinical feature), the 'patients' behaviour frequently led to a characteristic cycle of events – rising tension in the family followed by a period of severe distress for the relatives and culminating in a social crisis, which led to readmission'. It was noted that very little preventive work was carried out, services being mainly of help only after a crisis had been reached.[23] Thus, under existing conditions, the impact of a mental illness as it affects public opinion, or social agencies, may be, from the practical point of view, quite different in nature from other medical emergencies involving physical illness.

Official bodies reflect the difficulties in defining a psychiatric case by the differing ways they define one themselves. For scientific purposes, such criteria as have been used denote that a person has been under a doctor or a government department. The World Health Organization has used the factors of absence from work, or the taking of legal or social action. None of these criteria, however, is a 'symptom' in the common psychiatric sense, nor is it like counting X 'cases' of pneumonia. The type of person you are, your educational background, the family you belong to – and many other things – may affect your degree of awareness that you are breaking down; even if you are very ill, you may try to carry on, trying to deny that you are in any danger; only mildly affected, you may seek medical help early. In both adult and child psychiatric cases a large number of different, essentially non-medical bodies may have been involved in a case before a doctor is called in. For this reason the psychiatric services have had to develop 'community' techniques, to make for coherence of action. As yet in our society it often remains a difficult area for precise definitions and official statistics.

On the other hand, what are the attitudes of primitive people to what we call mental illnesses? In simpler cultures all illness, physical and mental, is thought mental, but mental in a special sense. That is, all illness is due to supernatural forces. The 'simple savage' lives surrounded by evil spirits, magicians, devils, witches. He believes in possession. His scheme of things explains mental illness particularly well. The abnormal person is, indeed, 'not himself'. He has every right to act as though 'possessed'.

Again, the primitive theory of illness gives rise to fairly appropriate treatment: magic charms, songs and dances, invocation, ritual, confession, suggestion. All these are reminiscent of treatment techniques, for example music therapy, used in our own 'enlightened' culture. Bronislav Malinowski pointed out many years ago that the 'garden magic'* of the Trobriand Islanders had much common sense and good gardening contained in it, even if it was all couched in magical terms. Thus we need not be surprised to learn that native psychotherapy works. Indeed, a deviant may be welcomed back to his society after treatment more wholeheartedly in a primitive culture than in ours. Social cure is more complete. In the coming-of-age of psychiatry in the West, the concept of physical disease is, paradoxically, of prime importance and clearly distinguishes our medicine from that of primitive peoples.

Contemporary Western life has been to a very large extent stripped of the rituals and traditions that characterize primitive societies making them conservative and resistive to change. A hurried technical civilization seems to require social mobility of its members, and seems also to produce an informality in the relations between people and between people and events. As we have said elsewhere, 'highly aware', and 'highly conscious' are qualities we admire in people. These qualities imply an individuality, an independence and a separateness in a person, a self-containedness. Lévy-Bruhl coined the phrase 'participation mystique', for the relationship we have with the world when we are unable clearly to differentiate ourselves from it. This is a state of lessened definition of the ego-boundary, a feeling nearer to love than to psychosis however, a feeling of oneness with the world – of 'oceanic feeling', as Freud called it – which has its

*The Trobrianders believe that the supernatural is responsible for most things. All success in love, for example is a result of magic – even conception, for the Trobriander doubts that there is a connexion between intimacy and conception. They employ 'love magic', and a man will charm some food or betel nut and give it to a girl, or he will offer her a flower to smell that has had an aromatic herb put on it. The same kind of thinking controls Trobrian food production. While it is called 'garden magic', it is as effective and practical as giving a girl flowers may be. (B. Malinowski, *Argonauts of the Western Pacific* and *The Sexual Life of Savages*, Routledge, 1922 and 1932 respectively.)

roots in infancy, in the fusion of identity we had with maternal figures – a subject we will return to in the next chapter. However, amongst primitive peoples participation mystique describes an everyday relationship with the world, a more continuous inability to distinguish the inner world of human feeling from the outer world of natural events than is the case with us. Primitive mythology expresses how primitive man feels inside himself about birth or death, sunrise or storm, spring or floods. Such myths are neither merely a kind of explanation of events in the natural world, nor merely a reflection of primitive feelings. Jung said, in discussing the effects of myths and ritual, '... *there is a release from compulsion and impossible responsibility* which are the inevitable results of participation mystique.'[24] Folk-lore and fairy tales may charm us still, but we do not take them seriously. A Jungian would say that, like poetry, any impact they have on us is because of the universality of meaning that they embody. A form of words gathers up sequences of deeply felt meaning. Religions and rituals may be analysed as simply the elaborated remnants of the problems and solutions we found in our remote infancy. In addition man's relationship to his different 'deities' can be seen as replicating the child-parents situation, with astonishing parallels with our view of the origins of neurotic symptoms.[25]

But with the decline of religion and the accompanying loss of religious and other ritual, man in Western society is left to face the 'compulsion and impossible responsibility' of the affairs of life quite alone. He has to try to make use of the resources of his inner world alone, without illusion, without myth. He is more individual and responsible than the savage, but he has also lost a socially accepted *guidance* system for his feelings, rituals and myth that would give feelings form, and, in particular, a *structure of ideas that would extend feelings in time.* He no longer knows how long he needs to work through emotional upsets or changes, how long the whole of him needs to mourn or rejoice, how long he should be dutiful, and when he should seek release from the obsessionality of his everyday life, which is so often more obsessional, trivial, yet onerous, than any religious life. Without puberty rites, adolescence gropes uncertainly through a decade or more before adulthood is reached.

Without feast days, or fasting, with few sexual taboos, our

contemporary concerns in nutrition and sex are obesity (and depression), diets, contraception, and a striving for sexual climax, rather than a gratitude for harvests or a veneration for fertility. We are perpetually seeking to be entertained or distracted by others or through the mass media, briefly to lose ourselves, rather than really to find ourselves, at any significant level. Laughter is, of course, abreactive. Through it we can release our tensions and aggressive feelings, on the whole harmlessly. But laughter gives few of us clues as to why we felt tense or aggressive. It brings a sense of well-being rather than being. And perhaps excepting athletics, music and art, our contemporary 'carnivals' are often far too brief to bring true catharsis. We may need to seek the long rituals of psychotherapy instead in order to find ourselves – in order to get in touch again with our own instinctual lives.[26] Of course, pagan mythology not only survived the impact of Christianity, but even partly took it over,[27] even ritually. Our Christmases have little to do with Christianity. In many ways we have inherited the disadvantages of ancient mythology, with its inherent ability to blind us to many of the truths about the physical and human worlds.[28] But it seems to me that it is in having preserved the special time-sense of primitive ritual, the perhaps days-long build-up to emotional crescendo, that the individual in a primitive society can often remain in better touch with his instinctual life. He does not expect instant cure of his ills, for example, but rather a ceremony. Even if the content of his myths seems nonsense to us, and even if we must avoid being senti-mental or idealizing about simpler cultures, which can be cruel and foolish enough, we ourselves have only recently returned to the idea that major mental illness can be treated, that this takes a long time, and that behind the illness and buried in it there remains the same social being as ourselves.

Loss of ritual and failure to separate the idea of a person from the idea of his illness may make us cruder than the 'savage' when it comes to mental illness. Some societies accept mental illness and its cure as natural far more than we do, even though they see it as an illness caused by the supernatural. We, on the other hand, are only at the beginning of studying our own society; while it is easier to ask questions than to supply answers, some answers are accumulating. There are many more to come. Our problems are not stated in terms of intractable devils, mysterious magicians or possession; it should be easier to devise increasingly subtle and searching techniques of social research, than to placate an angry goddess.

We have no reason to suppose that nowadays more people are becoming psychotic. The growth of psychiatry in the United Kingdom is evidence of improving care of mentally ill people, not of more madness. In the nineteenth century the apparent marked increase in the numbers of insane people merely reflected the fact that the Lunacy Acts of the time demanded registration of patients. Improved facilities for treatment contacted larger numbers of sick people.[18] Thus, as regards the genesis of major mental illness, our culture has not become markedly more malignant than it was – nor has it become less so. We continue to have severe problems in the care and rehabilitation of patients because of public attitudes towards the mentally ill. We are a multiple society, and so these attitudes vary greatly. The lowest status group may feel it has been environment alone that has overwhelmed them. Higher groups may be more aware of inner emotional forces in conflict. Members of the one group may keep their illness as secret as they can – feeling guilty, moral failures; in another group it may be possible to talk about symptoms and even to think it smart to have your own psychiatrist. In each case, the course of a mental illness may be altered because of the social setting in which it began. A slight deviation may be battered into roaring madness. A fairly severe disorder may be contained. At any rate, we find that the lower social classes tend not merely to have a higher incidence of mental disorder, but that it also tends to be more severe amongst them.

Nearly half the beds in the National Health Service – that is, 160,000 – are for the mentally ill. Even this is thought to be a poor guide to the number of mentally disordered people in this country. In one family in five, one of the members will suffer a disabling mental illness in his lifetime. One person in every fifteen in our country (one in eight of those over forty) will enter a mental hospital before they die. Figures of mental hospital populations are changing rapidly, due to new methods of managing patients. Only a very few years ago, however, it could be stated that four-fifths of patients in mental hospitals would stay

there more than two years. A third of those patients would be
schizophrenic. All these facts make the question of what constitutes a case from the community's (as apart from the psychiatrists') point of view supremely important. What leads to the
tolerance or intolerance of an individual? What are the details of
social rejection? In this chapter, we have tried to examine various
facts associated with the social recognition of mental illness. In
the next few chapters we will try to understand psychotic experience itself, trying to relate, among other things, the effects of
maternal deprivation or bereavement, which we have not considered here, to the expanding experience of early childhood.

Part Two

4 Stages and Hazards in Personality Formation

In the next few sections of this book I would like to go into the feeling states of the psychotic in a more detailed way. To do this we will take a more psychodynamic view of mind than the one employed generally in the chapter on classical psychiatric labels.

This new view developed because it makes sense of much that might otherwise seem nonsense. It verbalizes the non-verbal; it is an 'as–if' system. In describing mental life we share in a way the problem of the art critic. In one sense a painting only exists as daubs of paint in two dimensions; or one says, 'This is a picture of a King or Queen.' However, the art critic responds verbally to a work of art. He turns brush strokes, a tilt of the head, a gesture of the hand, into phrases; each feature of the painting becomes drawn into a pattern of thoughts and feelings which can be communicated. The critic's responses are 'as–if' the picture itself had become words. In our turn, we wish to reduce the apparent distance between the psychotic patient and ourselves. We will try to do this by claiming that the remoteness of the psychotic's experience from our present internal experience is largely a measure of our remoteness from our own infancy. And if we can feel our way into the infant's world, we must be using some primitive parts of ourselves to do so. To name these feeling parts of ourselves is interesting for it entails naming what once existed, and to an extent still exists, but has been nameless and wordless.

Let us say that we have no illusions about the 'objects' and 'structures' we will describe. They are convenient terms. They are not 'things', like nerves, or parts of the brain. 'Good and bad objects' are just words we apply to feeling states, so that we can talk about what people 'unconsciously feel'. This, too, is a 'label system'. It links together a very considerable amount of clinical, and a growing amount of experimental material.

All people, those who seem to deviate psychotically from us, as well as those who do not, have unconscious phantasies about what is in their body or mind. A phantasy is not necessarily part of an illness. A woman's handbag often stands unconsciously for the inside of her body. It may be untidy and full of weird rubbish; or it may be neat and tidy. She is obviously much too upset, however, when it is accidentally tipped out for it only to mean a handbag to her; but we need not call her phantasies about her handbag an illness. Phantasies seem to accompany biological drives. We are startled by an hallucinating adult; we are not used to this. Yet we are usually much calmer watching an infant suck-ing his fingers. It seems reasonable to say, on reflection, that the baby believes he is sucking a breast. This is his phantasy. This is, as Freud said, a baby's 'hallucinatory wish fulfilment'. The so-called defences, or mental mechanisms we will discuss – introjection, projection and so on – are merely ways of classifying the function of our phantasies.

(A) THE EARLIEST SOCIAL SITUATION

In this chapter I wish to discuss some of the emotional develop-ments of very early childhood, because of the light they can throw on the form and content of madness. In thinking about our-selves developmentally, we can come much closer to the psychotic person. He is, in a way, very much like we all were before we grew up, in the unremembered parts of childhood.

How is it then that we are in general so fearful of and alienated from the severely mentally ill? Can we argue that the strangeness of their experiences – the voices they hear, the beliefs they have which 'no one in his right senses' can share, their apparently groundless feelings of exaltation, apprehension or despair – is all to be found in the unremembered parts of infancy?

The mentally ill have problems both in relating to other people and in communicating their experiences to them. If one says to a distressed friend, 'I know how you feel', this can be a great comfort. This acceptance of the reality of another person's feelings (the basis of all psychotherapy) is constructive too with the psychotic. Our purpose is to get closer to his feelings. Let us then use our knowledge and understanding of early infancy to try to construct a bridge between ourselves and the psychotic.

Unaided, we cannot remember the first few years of life, even though in terms of the development of our personalities these were our critical years. This is in itself interesting, and must be gone into. To attempt to reconstruct our mental life from the beginning we must go back to a time before we had words. Thus we can only imaginatively and intuitively reconstruct the preverbal era from therapeutic work with children – or adults. As Melanie Klein has put it, we are dealing with 'memories in feelings'.[1]

We must put these memories as far as possible into words in order to be able to talk about them. These feelings and phantasies are the language of the unconscious mind, but they have to be translated into the words of consciousness. We should free our imaginations and try to feel our way back to the past. If we have ever been sad, when were we first sad? When did we first feel 'got at' or persecuted?

Looking at a baby in his first few weeks of life, we can think of him having – as we have – an inner and an outer world. He has no words to give precision. He has no sense of time to relate the appearance and disappearance of objects, to going away with the idea of returning. There is in his waking time a vivid here-and-now-ness about what happens – a world without words or time. He has limited means of testing reality and discovering what it might be. He is asleep for most of the day, and on waking he is not only hungry; all the sensory organs – sight, smell, touch – for many months mainly dormant in the steady state of the dark, warm womb, now pour their sensations into his awareness. He is like an overloaded computer in which the data fed in has not been properly coded. He will take days, weeks, months, to deal with these feelings, to identify and tabulate them.

Such is the simplicity of these early days that the baby cannot at first distinguish himself from the outside world. The me – the ego – and the not-me – the outside world – only gradually appear as separate ideas. In the early weeks and months the mothering figure is part of the baby's mind. Mother and child form the unity of feeling that one sees in classical statues of a madonna and child. The interaction in detailed emotional terms is very complex.[2] By six or seven months the infant has made an attachment of the most profound kind to his mother, and prolonged separation from her from this time on can be emotionally catastrophic.[3]

What are the contents of the primitive mind in these early weeks? Among the confusion, there is probably a need for a tender relatedness of a meaningful kind, even though the world may seem like a mere extension of the infant's own will.[4] Phantasy mingles with facts. There are exchanges between the inner feeling world of the infant and the world out there. The baby breathes in and out, sucks milk, voids. If frustrated, he reacts with violent anger. His feeling range is limited to anger, pleasure, pain and fear. Only slowly does he learn about whole people. At first he seems to know only unconnected parts of people – the breast that feeds him, faces, hands. And powerful feelings, uncontrolled, unexpressed by words.

In these early months of life it is as if there are only good or bad things present now, this instant. Good things can be taken inside. When the baby is hungry and feeding, milk is good and can be taken from the outer world into the inner. Both worlds feel good places. But hunger may be frustrated. The child cries out and makes angry movements. The inner and the outer worlds are bad. Survival itself depends on a hateful world. Repeated again and again through the early months, good experiences of gratification, and bad ones of frustration, build up attitudes in the infant towards his inner world. In each case his feelings are supreme; he is *omnipotent*. That is to say, his loving when he loves is a total feeling of commitment; and when 'persecuted', he has for a moment no inner or outer area of safety at all.

It takes time, then, and the development of the infant's mind to put the feeling qualities of things together in himself, and to see them as belonging to the same things. It takes time to see that the loving satisfying breast, and the hated frustrating one, are one and the same. The time this takes will depend on the maturity of the child at birth, his intellectual endowment and the quality of his emotional development. To make these ideas more real we should remember the passions of a small child, the urgency of his crying and the avidness of his feeding.

What has been achieved by now? As we have said, the baby

knows, in some sense of the word 'know', that he is the same infant when he loves as when he hates. He has an idea, in other words, of himself as a continuing person and of other people as continuing people. He knows that it is the same object that he loves and hates. The same person can appear to be hating or loving him. It is from this conflict that the earliest form of depression arises. This is the first dilemma of love versus hate. The child has taken inside himself the idea of a whole loving person – but he feels unable to protect that inner world person from the savage feelings also in his inner world. How the infant can stand this situation depends on whether he can believe his love is greater than his hate – or his hate than love. Here maternal care, past and present, must influence the effects of these feelings and the strength of the feelings themselves. The 'repeated consolatory experience'[5] of rescue from discomfort and hunger by the caring mother is the first creative social situation in our lives. When love is greater than hate, it can be used to overcome hate. It can keep alive memory, the belief in one's continuing ability to love and be loved in a real world, offering, if sadness now, promises of hope.

In the depressive illnesses of adult life or childhood, the primitive angry impulses and phantasies of our inner world become greater than the loving ones. The memories dominating the sick person's mind refer back to the aggressive feelings and phantasies of remote times, when as a tiny child he felt helpless, felt his love to be less than his anger and himself prey to destructive, depressive anxieties, with other shades of feeling – guilt, remorse, regret. These are the sort of words from our adult consciousness that we must impose. Just as an angry child feels totally evil so a depressed child or adult believes that only bad can be expected of him. He can only do wicked, dangerous things. An adult may commit suicide with these feelings, as though to protect others from his badness.

Most of the developments I have described happen unconsciously: our defences against depression also arise unconsciously. The mentally healthy and mature person has successful defences against depressing situations. He grieves over losing someone he loves – and recovers in time. In him, love is greater than hate. Reparation is believed to be possible after a destructive experience.

The analysis of depressed children and adults, however, brings up memories of love and hate of a different kind, where there is no hope, where hate seems to have won, is final, and cannot be overcome. The early stages of infancy are, of course, mostly concerned with a feeding situation. Everything goes to the mouth. The phantasies of the depressed are then oral. This will become clearer as we examine this model of a mind in more detail. Indeed, these states have been unequivocally called Psychotic Positions when first outlined as a description of normal infant emotional development.[6]

When we spoke of a child taking into himself good – or bad – things from the outer world and taking them in in a strongly emotional way, we were using the idea of *introjection*. The mother is at first perceived and recorded in the child in a fragmentary way – as a breast, or a face. Only at a later stage is a whole maternal person drawn into the child, or introjected. This mental mechanism of introjection can be seen as a special form of identification with an aspect of the environment,[7] as though the infant could meet his need to control and keep the source of all pleasure, his mother, by setting up inside himself an image of her, which then becomes part of himself. As for feeling the world outside to be bad when he is frustrated, this is an example of *projection* – a mechanism which operates in order to expel unpleasant feelings from inside himself by referring them to the outside world, being sure they originate and operate out there rather than from within.

It follows that if the infant uses these two mental mechanisms, these two ways of dealing with emotionally charged experiences, he will often have difficulty in distinguishing himself from the outside world. Projection, referring feeling to the outside world, and introjection, taking in, incorporating things in himself, make it harder to tell the *me* from the *not-me* in a realistic way. The mental world of early childhood is no simpler than madness.

Until fairly recently analysts have been reluctant to deal with psychotic patients. They had been warned by Freud that the special emotionally invested relationship – transference – did not develop between the therapist and his, say, schizophrenic patient, as it does with neurotic patients. Freud gave but passing reference to introjection in his New Introductory Lectures (1933). Yet the great clinician could not give up all hope. In his last book,[8] he said, 'We must renounce the idea of our plan of cure upon psychotics – renounce it for ever perhaps, *or only for the moment*, until we have discovered some other plan better suited for that purpose [my italics].' It has been shown, however, that it is often by projection and introjection that the schizophrenic, for example, communicates with his social situation, just as the tiny child does. The schizophrenic is frequently as uncertain as a child of his identity, and for the same reasons. He refers some of his feelings to the outside world one minute, and the next he assumes that things out there are part of himself. The borderline between me and not-me is broken. The ego-boundary is uncertain.

Again, keeping in mind that we are using a synthetic descriptive system rather than speaking of essential or total causes of mental illness, let us re-examine the infant's normal development, using the terms introjection and projection.

From the beginning, then, the infant introjects things into his simple ego. These things are good when they are what he needs, bad when they fail him. They can feel threatening to him because he projects his own aggressive feelings into them and then sees them as actually dangerous. He therefore sees these bad things as persecutors and he uses the imagery of his primitive feeding-dominated state to give content to these feelings. Thus he thinks his persecutors may devour him, or cut him up, or poison him. They even threaten the good images which are in his ego already. This kind of feeling we can call persecutory anxiety.

The ego is at first elementary. It is made up of the sensations of physical functions. At the beginning things to do with feeding loom largest; later the excretory functions grow more important, and so on.[9] From the start psychological defence mechanisms seem to exist to preserve the ego, or the emotionally charged good things which have been taken into the ego. (As we have said, these good things are only parts of things at first – a breast, a face, a hand.)

Projection and introjection are two such defence mechanisms. They are required to deal with anxiety, to minimize it, to maintain, if possible, gratification and pleasure, to keep control of an ever-changing emotional situation. One of the earliest defences is that of denial. By denial, we mean denial of psychic reality – a

kind of refusal to admit the true state of the internal world because it is too frightening or unpleasant. If denial should go on
to the denial of external reality, it could form the basis of a severe
psychosis in childhood or adulthood. Such a picture, with projection dominating relationships, can be seen in the paranoid
patient, who feels continuously persecuted, believing the world
is against him, having flung all his own unbearable anger out into
the world. Less intense persecutory anxiety lies behind the dread
of magicians, witches, or evil beasts, in children or superstitious
adults. The bad in us is referred out of us.

In a depressive psychosis on the other hand, the basic feeling is
one of loss. The loss is either that of a real loved person, or the
experience of an event which has had the same emotional significance as the loss of a loved person.[10] As we said earlier, it is as
though the first normal depressive 'illness' of infancy had re-
emerged and burst into adult consciousness. We will discuss in
another chapter some differences between normal mourning and
melancholia, and how mourning can be creative.[11]

In particular, this unremembered part of our very early childhood shares with the psychotic the problem of making contact
with reality, of distinguishing the self from the other, of phantasy
from fact. In infancy we experience the first emotional settings
in which we begin to learn about reality, and in which failure to
learn might leave an enduring nucleus of dynamic instability. If
there is a failure to learn, the challenges of later life – adolescence,
marriage, child-birth, bereavement, the 'change', or senescence –
could release again the phantasies and primitive anxieties that the
non-psychotic can barely bring back to mind. It is in these very
early stages, therefore, that the infant mind is a model of the
psychotic illnesses of later life. Here, in the infant, a being very
much of his body, with physical and emotional experiences going
vividly together, with images of creation and destruction and of
fragmented experience, with intensity and drama, is gathered up
some of the content and form of madness.

(B) THE ORIGINS OF FEELINGS OF PERSECUTION

The term *schizoid* was introduced into psychiatry to describe what
was often found to have been the prepsychotic personality of the

schizophrenic.[1] This personality has been characterized as asocial, serious, overtly cool and eccentric; timid, over-sensitive, or nervous and shy people have also been labelled schizoid. Personalities showing pedantry, suspiciousness, fanaticism, and callousness have received the same title. Such personality deviations may produce, in one social situation after another, a feeling of failure of communication, an increasing sense of inadequacy and of apartness. The schizoid feels split off from other people, just as his behaviour seems maladjusted to us.

It has been seen, therefore, that many schizophrenics were unusual people before we could actually call them mad. It can be argued that it would take only an exaggeration of schizoid traits to produce schizophrenia. By continuing to develop some ideas about very early childhood, we can forge more links to understanding psychosis, using now this word schizoid, but using it to describe a normal stage in infancy.

Persecutory anxiety is one of the earliest forms of anxiety. The first year of infancy can be divided into two phases. The first three or four months of life, we can call the paranoid-schizoid position. Not until the end of this phase does the infant come to recognize and experience its mother as a whole person. The remainder of the first year of life, that is, from the age of three or four months until about twelve months, holds interest for us in that the infant now knows a whole person rather than fragments of them. Some of an infant's feelings about a whole person can resemble both the feelings normal adult people have when they mourn, and also the feelings of a depressed psychotic.

Our concern is, of course, with phantasy as well as reality. We have said that the psychotic seems to experience a different reality from our own. An infant relates to all those experiences that seem real to him. His primitive mental and perceptual organization makes his reality different from ours. He is capable of experiencing anxiety from the beginning and has ways of defending himself against it.

There are two special emotional problems for him: one is in relation to life; one in relation to death. We need not invoke a 'death instinct',[2] this remains a controversial idea. It is worth noting, however, that in an average year in the U.K. nearly 6,000 people commit suicide, while only about 140 murders are committed. This suggests that in our culture a disturbed individual can turn against himself very much more readily than against another. We can say, at any rate, that any baby animal experiences the problem of survival: fear of extinction on the one hand, and a strong drive to develop and mature on the other. Going with a threat to life are the experiences of being cold, hungry or alone. Associated with life are love, warmth, feeding and tender handling.

When severe anxiety is produced by what is felt to be a threat to life, part of the anxiety can be projected. Part of it can also be converted into aggression, aggression against the infant's phantasized 'persecutors'. Hence an infant's crying becomes angry when he has cried too long.

And just as external reality is divided into black and white, good and bad, so is the ego. For at the same time as the fear of death calls forth projection as a defence, the drive for survival and for life creates a need in the infant for a countering phantasy of an 'ideal object', a perfect symbol, even though this is only, in the early stage, a fragment of his mother.

Relationships are therefore established between the infant and a good phantasy and a bad phantasy. This *splitting* of experience into stark contrasts is the most striking feature of responses to anxiety in the first few months of life. It is because of the huge differences, the total incompatibility of these phantasies, that we speak of 'splitting of the ego'. Anxiety is projected on to objects outside the child, and these objects are then felt as persecutors. A perfect image is also created from the need for good in the dangerous world of the infant. The experiential fragment of the infant's mother, which is magically evil, poisonous and threatening, or equally magically generous, bountiful and life-giving, is her breast. Bad experiences reinforce one image; good experiences reinforce the other. In a bottle-feeding society the infant can invest emotionally in a symbolic representation of the breast in the intimacy of early feeding, as it can with the breast itself.[3] Part of the mother feeds or does not feed; brings life to the mouth, or withholds life; part of existence, which can only be understood by the infant in terms of orality, of mouth feelings, is bad, or good only. There is no compromise, or gradation; existence is as split as night and day.

This first post-natal phase of life has been called, therefore, paranoid-schizoid,[4] because it is characterized by *persecutory anxiety*, like paranoid schizophrenia, and because the ego and the phantasies in the ego are repeatedly undergoing splitting. That is, they are schizoid.[5]

We are, of course, concentrating our attention on anxiety and responses to anxiety, and taking for granted that these are but special moments in the life of a normal infant who is otherwise sleeping or being played with, or feeding happily.

The main anxiety, when it occurs, is that the ego and the 'ideal object' will be overwhelmed. It is this that brings in one defence after another. The self strives to introject good experiences, and to project bad ones. Splitting of the ego permits the separation of persecutory phantasies from ideal ones, lest the one damage the other. Variations can be made in the use of defences, in what is taken in, or referred to the outer world. The aim is reduction of anxiety and preservation of those images that stand for life itself. Persecution, seeming to come from the outer world, is felt as a threat. When persecution is experienced in the inner world, it can be experienced as hypochondriasis, so much is the infant 'in his body'. And we should remember here the bizarre hypochondriasis of some schizophrenics.

There may be a kind of oscillating loving and hating, a swift alternation between wishing eagerly to feed, and suddenly being frightened, turning the head away from a breast that seems suddenly dangerous, as the defences swing. This foreshadows the paranoid schizophrenic, 'unable to keep a good object', whose interpersonal relations keep breaking down as he suddenly becomes suspicious, as he wonders 'What are their motives?' and 'Why are they being nice to me?' The paranoid keeps splitting inner and outer worlds.

The creation of an ideal object in the face of a high level of persecutory anxiety can become joined to a kind of omnipotent denial. The anxiety itself can then be denied: denied in the special sense in which we have used the term. Here is the picture of the wonderful baby who never cried – one in fact to whom all experiences were equally good, because of his preoccupation with a phantasy of good, and his denial of his own fears. The roots of an adult schizoid personality can be found in omnipotent denial and idealization of this order; at its most intense such denial reminds us of the thought disorder of the schizophrenic when he 'over-includes', so that he seems unable to differentiate between the relevant and the irrelevant, and all categories of experience melt into each other, all themes interpenetrate one another; he may smile fatuously, as, nursing his phantasies and ignoring our concern, his unreal or enigmatic answers emerge. We feel he is 'not all there' and think he is 'out of his mind', when really he is too much *in* his mind, and we are, to him, hardly there.

Introjection is a special form of identification. We can also speak of *projective identification*: '... the process which underlies the feeling of identification with other people, because one has attributed qualities or attitudes of one's own to them ... a patient's feeling that he *actually* is Christ, God, a king, a famous person ...'[6]

Here an aspect of the self is split off and projected, as though by doing so one could get closer to another, avoid separation, or gain control over them. The infant – or the psychotic – can project bad parts of himself in an attempt to be rid of them, or to attack an outside object. He may, in turn, fear retribution. Or he can project good parts of himself – cherished images – to keep them safe, as it were, when they seem to him to be threatened by destructive forces in his inner world. Now he may feel he has lost his goodness.

If all these different way of trying to master anxiety should fail, only a disintegration of the ego is left as a defence. In this, a damaging experience for the ego, the self, is projected as many fragments and identified with. (See page 86)

*

Chaotic though all these responses to anxiety may seem, the schizoid mechanisms we have outlined, which split the self and its images into good and bad parts, do gradually build up a kind of order in the infant. We are left, as adults, with a tendency to see things as black and white, only achieving slowly the discrimination to see the greys. As for children, goodies and baddies are the stuff of their stories.

If, in early infancy, good experiences outnumber bad, the stability of the phantasy of a good self, with good things inside it, allows the ego to integrate, and allows the good and the persecutory phantasies to come together. Splitting of the self and of its objects lessens. Projection is less and less needed as a defence. The self becomes a more coherent whole.

Thus our descriptive system sees a child in the first few weeks of life, from the mental point of view, as a being easily capable of emotional disintegration. Yet the disintegration is not haphazard or passively experienced. Rather, it comes in certain forms, so that we can devise a descriptive system for it, even if a highly complex one. Again, we do not see the infant's responses to anxiety as an illness. Rather, they are forms of defence and will contribute to useful aspects of his later personality. Projective identification, for example, is the primitive form of the empathy of later life – the ability to put oneself in another's place. Yet to do this, to put phantasized parts of oneself into another person, may lead to the fear that these parts of oneself are controlled by an agency in the outside world. These are the origins of 'passivity feelings', the schizophrenic's ideas of outside control. Again, if projection has been used to put angry feelings into the outside world, a fear of retaliation may follow. This can result in the paranoid patient shouting angrily without apparent provocation and perhaps really afraid, expecting an attack. A solution may be to offer him a cigarette, if he smokes. Oral gratification at such moments can be a powerful tranquillizer.

To say that one 'humours a lunatic' is an old, unkind saying. However, the psychotic's phantasies should be acknowledged lightly, neither colluded with, nor argued against. This is the way to avoid increasing his anxiety still further. Phantasy is for him reality, and is felt as part of his essential self.

The delusional 'ideas of reference' (see page 41) that are found in schizophrenia can also be seen as the effect of projections, where unbearable internal experience is flung out into the outside world: doubts about sexual identity, or even sanity. The nurse from the Teaching Hospital had such doubts. Delusions of persecution can be seen as attempts by the patient to believe he is good, by feeling that someone else is bad. The patient splits off the parts of himself which give rise to guilt – homosexual impulses, for example, or even heterosexual ones, if more usual sexuality is believed to be bad by him. He projects these impulses into

someone else – or even into an institution or a machine; the
Freemasons, the C.I.A., a cyclotron, or the people next door. And
being able to deny the bad impulses are his own, the patient can
believe that he himself is good. But, as we said earlier, the result
of splitting, projection and denial in infancy – and in psychosis –
creates out of the projected bad parts of the self, external persecutors. And so the neighbours, or the television, or the unread
scrap of newspaper intimately and vividly call back to the schizophrenic, 'Homosexual', 'Anti-Christ', 'Prostitute', or whatever.

There are some other curious features of madness and infancy.
Any parent who has had several children knows that rivalry
between them is normal. It has proved important to separate
jealousy from envy. Jealousy can be said to have its accent on the
loss to another of love felt to be one's own due. It is a relationship
between whole people: one child, for example, wanting its mother
all to himself, finding it hard to share her with his siblings. In
general it involves at least two people other than the one who is
jealous. A jealous woman feels deprived of the love of a man she
loves by someone else. She is angry with the depriver, but she
still loves the man. Envy is also an angry feeling – the angry feeling
that another person has and enjoys something desirable that the
envious has not. The angry envious feelings, however, are here of
course directed against the owner of whatever it is that is desired;
the impulse is to take it away or spoil it. Envy is, therefore, felt in
relation to only one person, or to one part of a person. It is
more primitive than jealousy.[3]

The infant we are watching develop has not yet recognized a
whole person. He cannot yet be jealous. He can be envious,
though. Envy has its stress on spoiling. It is wanting a possession, or an attribute and, if frustrated, wanting then to damage
that attribute. It is an aggressive and greedy drive.

The infant does not only want an ideal symbol of his mother –
he wants to control it, as though he himself could be, in his
infantile omnipotence, the source of all goodness and love. If he
should, in experiencing anxiety, feel full of badness and envy the
perfect fragment that stands for his mother, he will project in
phantasy the spoiling parts of himself, parts he feels at that
moment to be bad, images of urine, of faeces, into the envied
phantasy of perfection. This is the basis of the very regressed

schizophrenic, wet and dirty, or of some children who soil themselves as an 'act of aggression' against their mother. The poorly nursed senile dement will take 'revenge' by wetting, so second childhood needs mothering too.

Very intense early envy upsets the development of the child. The schizoid mechanism of splitting is confused. Instead of being able to have extreme divisions between perfection and malignancy, between an ideal and a persecutor, the ideal is itself spoiled by envy. It becomes difficult to distinguish the bad object from the spoiled, good one. The infant cannot introject an ideal and identify himself with it. Ego development – progress and maturation of the self – is held up. A lesser form of envy is devaluation; hence the denigrating remarks of men who envy women, or women who envy men.

There is a kind of borderline psychotic, who particularly fears insanity and is terrified of going mad. In such patients it is as if in their babyhood powerful envy was split off and remained unconscious. It continues, however, to give rise to phantasies of spoiling loved things. It is therefore productive of guilt feelings, with the flavour of a psychotic past trying to break into the present. Let us take as an example a husband in a situation not rare in its complexity:

The boy had been referred to the clinic because he was having nightmares. As his father and mother discussed their home and their lives, they talked less and less of the boy and more of themselves. The father at first appeared the stronger personality in the marriage. The mother was quite obviously fairly severely depressed; she rather desperately conceded how much more effective her husband was than she herself. He not only earned a good living for the family, but could do all the household things better than she could. He was better and more methodical at housework. He beat her at cooking. The children behaved well with him but played her up; and he could even sew. The father would nod in agreement as she wrote herself off, point by point. He would look up suddenly, eagerly, as though for approval, and then equally suddenly become sheepish and hang-dog. It became clear that he had competed with her as a woman – and had won. He had destroyed her confidence in herself as a woman. Towards the end of the interview he made an impassioned, yet vague kind of speech, tortured and hurt, as though trying in some way to claim a kind of special innocence he did not feel really his due; and, in strange contrast to all the talk of his superiority, there was his fear of breaking down, a fear which conveyed terror of an unknown chaotic future, yet which had a texture of familiarity to him. He lamented the risk of his losing some special gift or power, as a mere hint of a psychotic symptom, but nothing more.

Each sought in each other things denied them in their childhoods by others – he, his mother, who had rejected him; she, her father, who had died. She was mature enough to have become consciously depressed in her chronic but real unhappiness. He lived on the borders of disintegration. In his unconscious envy of her femininity, guided and compelled by phantasies of possessing and controlling the sources of all maternal goodness and love, he devalued his wife by acting as though he were the mother of the family, sensitively guided to his wife's vulnerabilities by his adult intelligence and his revengeful, infantile, destructive dreams. And, as his phantasies seemed to be carried out in reality, as his wife broke down fragment by fragment, his guilt grew. Yet neither saw each other as they really were. He stood unconsciously for her father, the protective provider towards whom she had unresolved hostility, as the father who had deserted her by dying. This hostility she could not express, admit, or recognize, but could only turn on herself. He had had to create, possess and control in his inner world a 'perfect breast' to envy and attack decades before his marriage fell about his ears, before his envy of femininity beat his wife down before his bewildered eyes. And, as his guilt grew, the anxieties that threatened to break free were psychotic ones, threats not just to images set up in his ego, but also to the integrity of his ego itself; the mechanism of splitting grew on the phantasies it fed on.

In more normal infancy, good mothering, love and care weakens envy. We can use an ordinary word for the internal counter to envy – gratitude. One of the most important attributes of love is the capacity for gratitude that it brings. Infants learning to love as they are loved experience gratitude as they construct more realistic relations with their mothers. Gratitude in this early form underwrites the appreciation of goodness in others and in oneself.[3]

We said earlier in this chapter that disintegration of the ego could be the only defence left, should all other defences fail, and that this is very damaging to the ego. It is an abnormal defence, invoked when all experience of reality is felt to be persecutory. It is a truly pathological form of projective identification, in which the self is fractured into multiple pieces in an attempt to erase all internal or external experience. The self and its contents are violently broken up and the split fragments projected in hatred. Yet, because of the nature of projection, the defence, far from lowering anxiety (which is the normal aim of defences) creates many new, threatening objects in the outer world. Reality, for this can be reality for a psychotic child, becomes even more unbearable. This also explains the acute, excited catatonic schizophrenic, emptied of identity, surrounded by many different threats of death, with no ego-boundary, no differentiation between himself and imagined horror, or himself and an infinitely hostile environment. This is indeed the '*autisme pauvre*' which in an earlier chapter we said could be understood differently.

Patients who are less ill may manage to preserve a 'third area',[7] to split off some relatively healthy remnant of the ego and with it some fragment too of the cherished, loved and loving, ideal object. In splitting these from the chaotic rest, some contact with a socially shared reality is possible. There will be something more of a familiar person left, and less alienation between him and us. Perhaps there will be, for him, a little less despair.

In the chapter on Cultural Influences we discussed how child-rearing practices vary in different human groups. This means that adults in different countries have vastly different attitudes towards children. Before a woman conceives she already has largely learned feelings about intercourse, pregnancy and childbirth. She is certain that scolding or cuddling or swaddling is good for babies. The differences are not merely ones of language but also of handling, body contact, warmth or distance.

All newly born babies cry in the same way, but already, by five or six months, the sounds they make have moved appreciably nearer to the language of their culture.[8] In the same way, but harder to measure with exactness, the influence on the child of different parental attitudes towards feeding, weaning, toilet training and all the other emotionally loaded aspects of early life – emotionally loaded both for parents and for child – varies. Family studies are emerging, but they have yet to achieve the apparent sophistication of intensive, individual studies. One individual can supply so much puzzling, fascinating data. The problem of handling a family group, of following all the rapid emotional exchanges and patterns, even with the help of cameras and tape-recorders, can be truly staggering. Yet we have reached a point in psychiatry where 'a major theoretical problem is the relationship between the social structure and individual experience'.[9]

Bernstein, whom I have just quoted, regards speech 'as the major means through which the social structure becomes part of individual experience'.

A child does not speak much until he is about two years old. Yet even if his noises are now more English or more Hindi, or whatever, than they were, they are not words as we know words. Non-verbal communication is still his way of receiving and transmitting information. If we restrict verbal communication to any meaningful definition, it will largely exclude baby noises, even if very different cultures are being pressed home in very different words by a parent of one culture or another.

A final schizoid mechanism[10] is often found in the families of schizophrenics.[11] The authors of the study *The Psychodynamics of Family Life*[12] give an account of their experiences with the families of young hospitalized schizophrenics. They found working with such families a disturbing experience, despite their own expertise. They reported an elaborate but mostly hidden disturbance affecting the whole family: by long-established habit, the individual members kept up 'stereotyped models' of their family roles, which complemented those of the other members in that the family group interacted to maintain their disturbance and colluded in the denial of the anxieties generated by this. Such a family would be of this kind:

The clinic had become involved, because Gerald's mother rang for an appointment. Gerald had been treated there for night terrors as a five-year-old. The night terrors had responded well to treatment and the case had been closed. At the time, the mother had been thought to have had a highly ambivalent attitude towards Gerald, and she was thought to be a chronically depressed woman. Gerald had an elder sister, but little was recorded about her, except Gerald's poor relationship with her. No comment had been made about the father, who had apparently not been seen. The new complaint was how aggressive the mother found Gerald, who was now seventeen. The mother was seen for a new social history, and the Psychiatric Social Worker found her again depressed. Gerald was seen by the psychiatrist. A tall, good looking, alert young man, Gerald gave a very reasonable account of himself. His parents quarrelled a lot he said. This upset him. He found it hard to say anything against himself, but he could say his father should be more in charge in the family, and should even support his mother when she corrected him. Gerald's mother criticized Gerald's friends, his clothes, she nagged him, she was unreasonable. All this sounded merely like an adolescent rebelling against parental control, the reasonableness of which could not yet be ascertained. It was unusual in that Gerald seemed to be praising of his father and hostile towards his mother, hardly the usual 'oedipal situation', with a boy rebelling against his father. The Psychiatric Social Worker saw Gerald's father separately. He was a skilled worker in industry, intelligent, but not very verbal. It was hard to get much of a feel of the family from him. He would not commit himself and seemed uninterested in the family or the problem. A joint family interview was arranged to see how all the members interacted.

Gerald and his father came in together in a friendly way. The mother came in a distance behind. The psychiatrist and Psychiatric Social Worker explained how they thought a joint meeting might help all present to see more clearly what the problem was. The father laughed and exchanged a knowing grin with Gerald. The mother changed colour and began to speak anxiously at high speed. Gerald had tried to eat her hair when he came to see her in hospital she said. Gerald and his father roared with laughter. Gerald urinated over the floor at home she said. Again the man and boy laughed. The Psychiatric Social Worker and the psychiatrist again and again tried to get the father or Gerald to confirm or deny things that the mother said. Gerald, if his attention was caught, merely fell silent and looked down at the floor. The father would reply by bringing out some anecdote or other to illustrate what an awful wife he had – how the house was never clean, how meals were always late or burnt. The mother was crying now, yet still ascribing incredibly primitive, infantile behaviour to her seventeen year-old son. She was certainly desperate, but expressing the despair of persecution, not of depressive anxiety alone. Her 'pressure of speech' increased and she began to have a strange fixed expression on a face still wet with tears. She began to speak of the mocking voices she heard. And as she did so, her husband and son still found it wildly amusing that this woman was hallucinating.

Seen alone, each member of the family had been quite different. Seen together, even the diagnosis of the mother changed. As a single person seeing a social worker, she had seemed depressed. Seen in her family group she appeared paranoid, and her description of the attacks on her by her son altered from one telling of his verbal rudeness, to one telling of her experience of this violence in infantile and symbolic terms – as attacks with bodily products on her or 'her house'. The clinicians could feel themselves becoming more and more angry and helpless, unable to understand or intervene, as the father and son continued as a pair sharing secret jokes, making allusions obviously devastating to the mother, yet socially meaningless without an understandable context. Not one particular event or incident would be talked about simultaneously by the mother, father and son. It was like a tank battle at night. The great flashes of violence were there. The objectives of the combatants however, were in darkness, and an extended diagnostic technique, the joint interview, had produced more questions than had existed before.

So strong were the emotional forces at work in these families that the psychiatrists sometimes felt later that at the time they had been drawn into the maze without noticing it. Often communication within the family disintegrated – yet the disintegration was ignored. There were gross emotional contradictions, and a silent annihilation of intent and meaning. Emotional experiences were habitually ignored and attempts by the psychiatrists to clarify them, or to verbalize feelings, were usually resisted. The families seemed to regard the idea of meaningful and real relationships with a shared horror.

The schizoid infant, too, can have a horror of links. Surrounded by disintegrated, hostile objects he may set out to destroy every link with his dangerous reality that he can. He withdraws from our shared reality. He will not connect a hand with an arm, a nipple with a breast, a face with a person. The psychotic child can 'over-impress' that other people do not exist. He can impress that they, somehow, *should* not exist. Beyond all the psychiatric jargon about 'interpersonal relations', the sight of the psychotic child is negative proof of the reality of the idea of 'relating' – for he visibly does not.

Nicola, 26 years old, had had first a period of severe insomnia, during which, if she slept, she had nightmares which had the directness of a child's dreams. She dreamt her home was on fire, and her mother and brother Jeremy were burned up. Another dream would be of her father and Jeremy being killed in a car crash. After several weeks of day-time over-activity, bad dreams and insomnia, her behaviour became incoherent. She showed the symptoms of acute excited catatonic schizophrenia, appeared to be unable to relate to those around, laughed inappropriately, and wept at times in a way equally unconnected with any real external events. She could no longer work and was admitted to a mental hospital.

Nicola's 'thought disorder' showed itself by 'blocking'– by her stopping suddenly as she was speaking. Her speech otherwise never made a point, yet it could now and then have a quality that made one particularly listen, as though she was about to tell you why she had broken down. The pressure of speech, the neologisms, the word-salads that mostly characterized her talking, however, prevented much two-way communication with her. After the first visit of her parents she became silent. At this time, for a few days, Nicola *cut off all links*, and remained almost stuporose.

Nicola's family consisted of her father, her mother and her brother Jeremy, who was aged 24. Her father was Welsh, one of a family of ten. He had always been the odd-one-out in his family. A self-employed, intelligent man, he seemed frustrated in some way. His wife, Nicola's mother, was a Londoner. She blamed Nicola's illness at first on the way her own mother had fussed and babied Nicola when she was small, preventing her, 'the real mother', from mothering her own child. It became clear as one talked to her that she still had a hostile, yet dependant relationship with her own mother, as real as though that person had not been dead these five years.

Nicola had seen very few other children before starting school at five, apart from her brother. She had been a tomboy as a child, whereas Jeremy had been passive, gentle and interested in dolls. While Jeremy even now had never been out with a girl, Nicola had had a few episodes of intense sexual curiosity and exhibitionism – vigorously put down – scattered through her childhood. This involved her in taking her, or other children's, pants down when she was small. Being rather religious and 'old-fashioned' as the father put it, the parents struggled very hard to eliminate this behaviour.

At a second interview with her mother it emerged that when Nicola's mother was late on in her pregnancy with Nicola, an elderly woman had committed suicide in the house. This was treated as a case of murder for a while by the police, and it had precipitated several months of anxiety in the mother, covering the period of the birth of her child, and being graphically expressed by Nicola refusing the breast at two months of age, and being very difficult to feed with a bottle, which she would only accept from her father. That is to say, the mother had been unable to shield her child from her own anxiety. The dominant grandmother lived with the family then, and in this second interview it came out briefly that the mother had been obsessed with the idea that 'the wrong person had died' in the suicide, that it should have been herself, or her own mother. She could not, at this interview, accept the idea that this 'obsession with an idea' might have been a wish, and in later interviews, refused to speak further about the incident, or even acknowledge that she had spoken of it.

Interviews with Nicola during this time showed her to be pre-occupied with three particular 'delusional' ideas. She thought she was changing sex. She believed her parents were not her real parents. She felt she herself was very old, but had just been reborn. While these ideas were delusional in one sense, in another they could be understood.

Her father, for all his religious notions, had always been a seductive figure to his daughter. He kissed and cuddled her and swung her on his knee when she was a child. He had little sexual intercourse with his wife and was often sexually frustrated. This showed itself in his eroticized relationship with his daughter. Yet if Nicola showed any erotic responsiveness, this was punished by both parents. They tolerated a tomboy daughter, however, or a passive asexual identity, such as the one Jeremy had had as a boy. Neither of these parents had a child-raising technique that gave a clear idea to a child what being a boy or a girl meant. And so in her adolescence, with the physical changes of the stage completely unexplained at home, Nicola always experienced full sexual feeling guiltily. There could never be affection without sex, and never sex without guilt. A series of affairs in her teens always ended in intercourse, to her bewilderment. While each parent claimed the family was a close one, Nicola had never felt understood. Each parent said she was a happy child, yet she looked back at an anxious, fearful childhood, in which her brave tomboyishness had been no mere expression of her envy of maleness, but nearer to a search for herself, a self, from her point of view, rejected as female. Just as her mother could not identify properly with her own aggressive mother, so Nicola failed.

The family had a clear view of what kind of family they were. The father prided himself on being someone the children could turn to when troubled. Yet Nicola feared him in fact, and found he had never seemed to believe in the feelings she tried to express to him. He was proud of her tomboy act in her girlhood – 'There's confidence,' he would say. Yet she had gone through agonies of uncertainty in an inner self, never in touch with her mother or father. It was indeed, for her, as though her parents were not her parents. She could, in a mad way, only please by changing sex. Now in her psychosis she was trying to be born again.

In the families we have just discussed, who is the patient? The young schizophrenic in hospital? The family? If communicating is as distorted as this, is it not better to retreat altogether, to become schizophrenic? And what of the genetic studies? How, in families like this, do we determine which is seed and which is soil?

(C) FEELINGS OF LOSS: MOURNING AND DEPRESSION

We let our infant struggle through a confusing world of anxieties and defences until he is three or four months old. By splitting his 'objects' and his own self, by projection and introjection, he sorts out his feelings and perceptions and separates good from bad. While we notice the difficulties of this primitive world, we must also see all this as a complex yet human drive towards an ultimate unity of mind, towards integration. If the baby feels that his own love and the 'loved object', the mother he has identified with, are stronger than his bad experiences and his own bad impulses, he will be better able to identify with his mother. Projection of his bad impulses will therefore be less frequent; he will be less afraid of these impulses and for this reason will need to project them less. He will also begin to recognize them as his own; splitting will be less often used. That is to say, denial, projection and splitting, some of the defences against anxiety that made it so difficult to tell the 'me' from the 'not-me' – the 'self' from the 'other', the infant himself from his mother – some of these defences become less dominant. In other words, the infant's ego becomes stronger and his ego-boundary gains in definition. He moves nearer to recognizing reality. Decisively, it is at this point in development that the infant recognizes his mother as a whole person. She is no longer seen as a 'part object', as the jargon has it – a hand, a breast, a face. He relates himself to a whole person.

We may remember the psychotic child, George, who still only related to fragments. He had never reached this point of mental development in early infancy, but remained almost inaccessible in the divisive feeling world of the stage before it.

Soon after relating to a whole maternal figure the normal infant begins to recognize other people, his father and so on. What does 'recognizing his mother', 'relating to a whole person' mean here? It means that the infant is *facing his own ambivalence*.

It means that he sees for the first time, at about the fourth month of life, that he loves and hates the same person.

A recent study[1] suggests that the reason that laughing in babies, as apart from smiling, only starts in the fourth month of life, is because ambivalence has not been developed until then. Laughter is a mechanism to reduce emotional tension. Laughing in an infant seems to be brought about by situations which simultaneously stimulate in him opposing tendencies. He wants the situation to go on but wishes it would stop. Tickling a baby in the first few weeks of life is most likely to produce only anger or fear. From sixteen weeks or so onwards, however, tickling produces both negative feelings in the infant and rather stronger feelings that he would like the tickling to go on. This mixture seems to produce laughing. While we are essentially concerned with feelings of loss and depression in this chapter, perhaps here we can see why the young schizophrenic, with his enormous problems of unresolved ambivalence, can meet one social situation after another in a fatuous, giggling way, being unable in his confusion to decide whether he wants the situation to continue or to end. A fatuous schizophrenic, then, has an infantile sense of humour. Similarly, adult gambling, or taking a chance of any kind, may both provoke and be a response to powerful omnipotent phantasies; but it is also a kind of plea for life to be less determined, less predictable. It is a cry against internal and external fate.

In discovering his ambivalence, the infant has so far only discovered his own helplessness and dependence. His feeling that the world is a mere extension of his will, his phantasies of omnipotence, have suddenly received a rebuff. He sees now that his mother can go away and that she can return again; it seems to him that he has no control over her any more. This is what Melanie Klein meant in talking of the 'depressive position' of this period, when the infant recognizes a 'whole object' and relates himself to it. He cannot yet have continuing faith in continuing good; he cannot yet 'take a chance' emotionally that the good in life will always return. He has no 'common sense' and no idea of probability, even though his good experiences have outnumbered the bad sufficiently for him to have created a precious point of reference for all feeling within himself.

In the earlier, paranoid-schizoid position his chief anxiety was that the ego itself might be destroyed by threatening objects experienced in phantasy. The characteristic bad feeling was persecutory anxiety. In the depressive position his main anxiety is that *his own angry wishes have destroyed, or might destroy, the phantasy of a loved object which has been created inside the ego*, this mother figure upon which life itself seems to depend. The characteristic bad feeling of this second psychotic situation is *depressive anxiety*. The only meaningful things in infancy are successions of intense egocentric emotional experiences. To reach mental health as an adult, somewhere along the line of development the real and the unreal must begin to be set more clearly apart from one another. After the self has been distinguished from the other, phantasy still rules the mind. The new involuntary despair must be overcome. How is this done? The infant increases his use of introjection. He tries in phantasy to take in repeatedly his ego-ideal, his mother, in order to avoid separation from her; he tries to protect her inside himself from the bad parts of himself. He is still a small animal, dominated by feelings of the mouth. He is like the young lover, saying to his love 'I could eat you.' But his imaginings seem to him so powerful that he fears that his ability to set up inside himself an image of what he loves, that the use, in other words, of the 'oral introjecting mechanism' will itself destroy not only the inner phantasy but also the figure which it represents in the outside world. For him an angry wish is a destructive act, an act as real as any other part of his experience.

And so new feelings arise, feelings of *mourning* and *pining* for the good object. They are also of *guilt*, stemming from the infant's conviction that he himself has been responsible for the destruction and loss. He believes his bad wishes have themselves destroyed what he loves. He has become aware of his ambivalence towards his mother figure and at the most tense moments of ambivalence he feels as though his internal object is in broken pieces, chewed up, crunched into fragments. It is as though his inner world is again at times in pieces. There is a powerful echo of the earlier period as he regresses, experiencing persecutory anxiety again and feeling threatened by incoherence and disintegration. At this stage his feelings are identical to those of a psychotically depressed adult.

But in normal infancy the full experience of depressive anxiety creates in time the wish to repair. *Reparative phantasies* begin to arise to counter the phantasies of destruction. Omnipotent creative phantasies move the infant out of the trap of melancholy.

... while grief is experienced to the full and despair is at its height, the love for the object wells up and the mourner feels more strongly that life inside and outside will go on after all ... suffering can become productive ... painful experiences of all kinds ... stimulate sublimations ... bring out quite new gifts.... The pining for the lost loved object implies dependence on it, but dependence of a kind which becomes an incentive to reparation.... It is creative because it is dominated by love, while the dependence based on persecution and hatred is sterile and destructive.[2]

This is then creative mourning; it is healthy, normal mourning. If this basic pattern of response to loss is laid down in childhood, it will determine the outcome of responses to feelings of loss in later life. After this first kind of mourning, the chance can be taken that life, after mourning, will be good again.

To sum up, reality-testing becomes more possible in the infant when his ego becomes basically more integrated and projection lessens. Perhaps his first clear human 'insight' is insight into the reality of his mixed feelings for his mother. It carries at the time the bitterness of apparent helplessness and dependence upon someone else. This insight will be lost again later, though the ambivalent feelings will unconsciously survive. For the first time the infant becomes aware of himself as a separate person from his mother. Through belief in his reparative abilities, phantasy and reality now move apart. Separateness, depression and creativity can interact. With the discovery that the inner world is a different and separate thing from the outer world, the infant's belief in the overwhelming force of his imagined destructive powers and wishes begins to lessen. He sees more clearly how some of his impulses are good and some are bad. He begins to notice his mother's survival of his bad feelings about her. He notices that his loving, which has begun to carry with it creative, repairing phantasies as magical as his old destructive dreams, can also only have a limited effect. Love and hate therefore have real limits set to what they can do. And the loving part of the child will be cherished by him as greater than the hating part. He will realize that love is greater than hate.

*

We have now reached a level of development with the infant where we can point to different outcomes for his future personality, depending on how he has managed to deal with his anxieties and to arrange his defences. In talking of the future we are restricting ourselves for the moment to possibilities of psychotic illnesses.

In studies of animal behaviour and development there has been interest in 'sensitive periods' and 'imprinting'. 'If a day-old chick or duckling hatched in an incubator is allowed to see any moving object, it may follow that object as it would its own mother and subsequently direct towards it many of the responses normally elicited by its parents ... the initial exposure must occur during a limited "sensitive period".'[3] That is to say, during a short part of their early life many animals are peculiarly open to learning very important parts of their behavioural repertoire. And experiments show that this learning can seriously miscarry, producing curious, comical, bizarre or even tragic maladaptations. Nothing can be stated quite so clearly yet about humans. Nevertheless, there do seem to be appropriate times to initiate weaning, toilet training, and so on. Later, or earlier, may be the wrong time. At the time generally considered to be right, learning not appropriate to the situation may occur because distortions in the environment interact with special vulnerabilities in the infant. The infant can only interpret these distortions within the bounds of the primitive perceptual apparatus he possesses; and he is guided by the kinds of anxieties we find difficulty in naming; he is using defences which are only prominent and obvious in us when we are mentally ill, or that can only be posited as the quality of early infantile experience.

We know, for example, from experimental work, that there is 'evidence for the beginnings of *form* perception within the first few weeks of life ... sensitivity to *patterns* within a form is hardly more delayed.' The infant prefers to look at patterns. 'One odd finding' is that 'the human infant does very much better with one eye than when using both together. The implication would seem to be that adult binocular vision, wherein information from the two eyes is integrated into a single perceptual world, depends upon learning or later maturation of the nervous system. For the baby, it seems that what is entering through one eye may very well interfere with what is coming in by the other.'[4]

We might well ask whether the biological basis of what we have called 'splitting' is to be found in the development of infantile perception – splitting of feelings into only good or bad ones, splitting of objects and of the self. Splitting may be based, then, on the imperfect perceptual apparatus of the first few weeks. Is it because of this apparatus that the infant relates to mere parts of objects – parts of people – these parts being all he can perceive? High levels of anxiety at this time might interfere with 'learning or later maturation of the nervous system'. Failure to mature here could therefore not only leave excessive levels of primitive anxiety, but this anxiety might also be associated with an arrest in perceptual development. Obviously physical factors yet to be identified could also intervene, preventing the evolutional development of either the early forms of anxiety or of perception. Equally, nature and nurture could malignantly combine to produce the same effects.

Take five-year-old Hastings – an illegitimate coloured boy. Following cardiac surgery in the first few weeks of life, he has been in a hospital ever since, where staff has repeatedly changed over the years. It is very difficult to find out about his earlier psychological development, since the hospital notes are only concerned with his physical state, and are scanty even there. He has had months-long episodes of banging his face with his fist since at least the age of three years. The face banging has led to thickening of the skin over his knuckles and to scarring of his face. The habit was 'treated' in hospital by splinting his arms and by sedation. The child psychiatrist examining Hastings found him a limp, speechless child, quite unable, apparently, to relate to him. He thought he could make no contact at all with the boy, until the nurse with the boy, who had been giving an account of the problem, mentioned the splinting. Hastings then began to bang his face. At first the psychiatrist restrained the boy, to protect him from himself, though feeling guilty for doing so, knowing how punitive restraint feels to children, and how aggressive it can make them. He had a cold and it struck him he could protect the child's face with one of his paper handkerchiefs.

In fact, when he put the tissue, rolled into a ball, on to Hastings's cheek, the boy stopped banging himself. He smiled, closed his eyes and leaned his face onto the soft ball of paper. He acted as if he had stopped punishing himself for 'destroying' the mother who had vanished, and in this psychotic moment hallucinated a wish fulfilment, a return of a breast-mother, not a whole person, but a breast standing for her, to which he can relate.

Sally, a little blonde girl of two and a half years, was equally unrelating. She was very agile and over-active, however, with a curious face frozen half-way between smiling and looking horrified. She seized hold of a coloured wooden disc from a set of pyramid rings and sucked greedily at the hole in the centre of the disc, accepting a mere disc of wood as a breast, phantasying a nipple. Not only did Sally do this (a variation on the response of babies to very simplified representations of their mothers faces[4]) but she also responded to the hole in the disc as though a breast and a nipple were quite separate objects which she could put together in phantasy, and needed to. She had, in her whirlwind exploration of the play-room earlier, shown an obsessive interest in cavities, cupboards, openings, all of which could easily have been interpreted in terms of birth phantasies, or sexually. Yet she seemed in retrospect to have been searching for an approximation to the object she could relate to: a breast imagined out of a disc of wood, a nipple from a hole the right size.[5]

Whereas with Hastings the environment had been always hopelessly against him, little of note could be found in Sally's family history, excepting that her father had made a short trip to the Far East when she was ten months old, and her mother had felt just a little insecure then. Until ten months Sally had been an eager, normal baby. Then she withdrew from whole people, quite quickly.

In terms of our model infant there are clearly possible 'fixation points' for psychotic illnesses, 'sensitive periods', as it were, when the nucleus of what our culture would call an illness could be laid down. Thus the *paranoid-schizoid position* we have discussed lends itself to being a *fixation point for schizophrenia* and the anxieties of the position can be linked to psychotic child or adult symptoms, as we have seen. Persecutory anxiety characterizes the tides of feeling of this state, a feeling response in a mind that can only, for a while, order its experiences by splitting, denial and projection. The *beginning of the depressive position* is a pattern of words we can impose on an infant's emotional evolution and also on a *psychotic depression*. The shorthand we use for the terrors of this state are depressive anxiety, a state of pining, mourning, guilt, and a special kind of pain. Regression to either fixation point would lead to the loss of the sense of reality we normally share with each other, to the 'unreal reality' of psychosis, the private nightmare, the hardly shared horrors of a breakdown. In the sense of symptoms of an illness the anxieties would then continue and become disabling. In normally developing infancy these are only phases, never completely worked through, to which are added other normal moments in growing up of reward and punishment. Significant life situations contribute to the emergence of symptoms of psychotic illness; there are also cultural influences, such as class or family; and *constitution*, that complex of physical and environmental accidents. And the physical dilapidations of time can release madness in the old. *Yet if the depressive position is at least reached and partly worked through in infancy, future emotional troubles can only be neurotic, not psychotic. This is because contact with reality and the ability to test reality have been established. Gradually the infant will be able to generalize his love from his mother to other people. He will feel more clearly responsible for his own drives and be able to bear reasonable guilt.*

*

Ours is a guilt culture. We know that depression and suicide are rare in some primitive societies; these seem to be cultures that have avoided our strong 'sense of sin'. Thus the Javanese, who put only minor restrictions on their behaviour, have little incidence of depression. The Chinese who live among them are much more 'guilt-regulated' and prone to depression. The Hutterite religious community we mentioned in an earlier chapter has a very high incidence of depression, four times higher than their rate for schizophrenia; theirs is a guilt-dominated community. We can conclude, therefore, that a high incidence of depressive illness is related to 'severe super-ego sanctions' in a society; that is to say, to a punishing conscience. We can trace the development of the super-ego, or conscience, in terms consistent with our infant model. If we do this, we will understand in more detail how mourning can miscarry and become a depressive illness.

The super-ego is at first a terrible phantasy; it is only slowly scaled down to the proportions of the control wielded by the real parents, so augmented has its power been by the additions and distortions of the primitive child's mind. A mind can be taught to feel guilt to an excessive degree, and while our parents' voices fade in us, their injunctions remain. And so we find that, after the charming, chaotic, maddening and endearing antics of the preschool era, a child begins to settle down and that as his responses to our control improve, so does his self-control. He enters the 'latency period', between the first tumultuous years and the explosions of adolescence. We wish to understand how it is that the super-ego can be so agonizingly relentless and punitive in some people. We wish to see why the acutely depressed psychotic wrings his hands in despair and calls himself a cruel failure, worthless, despicable. Feelings of this kind are sustained by phantasies created in infancy. Indeed, they are the phantasies of the early part of the depressive position of infancy where guilt follows on the phantasy of destructive wishes.

In Chapter 1 we discussed the ego and the unconscious mind, but left out a consideration of the super-ego. The unconscious aspect of mind we characterized as timeless, illogical, egocentric and amoral. It is without words, as the infant is, and its motives are simply the seeking of pleasure and the avoidance of pain. In a strange way, usually only familiar to us in our dreams, the energy of the feelings in this part of us can slip easily from one idea to another, so that a visual experience that is superficially innocent can bring only too credible joys or fears. It is in this unconscious part of us that we remain infantile, and crudely sexual, creative or destructive. It is to this part of the mind that we involuntarily dismiss ideas that seem too upsetting to our idea of ourselves when we repress them.

We have already followed some of the evolution of the self, the ego. In a way, the ego, in separating itself from the unconscious, does so in terms of opposite qualities. Developing through infancy and childhood, it derives largely from the unconscious, but it is itself logical, moral, conscious and related to reality and to the outside world. It becomes aware of time; and, of critical importance, it eventually has language in which to communicate with itself and the world. The ego remains unconsciously linked to the unconscious, acting in this way as an intermediary between it and the environment. It is an intermediary, however, not only between external reality and the drives of the unconscious; it is also acted upon by the force of the super-ego, by which it can be controlled or inhibited.

The super-ego itself derives from the ego, but because it is our internal morality, it has to function much more closely to the amoral unconscious, and so is much less accessible to us than consciousness. As our own internalized critic, it is the source of our sense of guilt. Freud called the super-ego the 'heir to the Oedipus complex', meaning by this that a conscience which resembles to a substantial degree that of a mature adult only emerges after a child has worked through the 'triangular problem' that it has with its parents. It therefore takes about five or six years for our consciences to begin functioning in this more adult manner. The Oedipus complex refers to the way in which a child is attracted to its parent of the opposite sex, seeing in phantasy the other parent as a feared rival. The super-ego owes its origin largely to the child identifying with the parent of the same sex and solving the problem of rivalry with them by 'identifying with the aggressor', as the child unconsciously feels that parent to be.[6]

The super-ego is created by the introjection in phantasy of the mores of the parents. This phantasy will be a distorted representation of the real parental figures, distorted because of the feelings the infant will have projected on to them. The roots of conscience can be traced back to the earliest situation, when first an ideal and a persecutory object were taken into the ego. The 'persecutory object' was experienced then as ruthless and retaliatory; and the 'loved object' was so perfect that it was to become an 'ego-ideal', an aspect of the super-ego containing a feeling of perfection so unattainable that it too could partake of an aura of persecutory feeling. As the ideal and persecutory objects came together in the depressive position, as splitting of objects and of the self diminished and the ego became integrated, so the super-ego too became more integrated. It began to be experienced as another 'internal object', sharing an ambivalent, love-hate relationship to the ego, just as the ego had with the real external mother. Acts going against the conscience therefore seem like acts taken against precious parts of ourselves, and awaken persecutory anxiety; threats to the integrity of the super-ego give rise to feelings of guilt and to self-reproach. It is thus that the guilt 'self-regulating system' works. This is the basis of our socialized behaviour, more effective for most of us than the police. As with other parts of us that can be traced far back in time, the super-ego takes as a model for itself body functions dominating the different phases of our upward-spiralling existence, which becomes progressively more complicated. The orality of earliest times give us not only one of our earliest patterns of love-loss, when we are weaned. Knowing about the angry feelings experienced at the time of pre-verbal 'language of feeling' of the mouth makes sense of the expression 'gnawing conscience', in that we can understand that these oral feelings attach to phantasies of people we set up within us in infancy. Some kind of awareness of the power to please or displease parents by controlling the bowels gives another even more powerful and cruel controlling quality to the developing super-ego. A military 'mopping up' operation is a euphemism for what is usually essentially sadism. Conscientious people don't like to make a 'mess of things'. The guilt of depressed people, which is our particular interest here, is a felt responsibility for phantasized murderous attacks, as though the depressed believed they had torn someone they love to pieces and despoiled and degraded them.

It was Freud who first linked manic-depressive insanity to the *grief reactions* we feel when someone we love dies.[7] He described the self-hatred and self-accusations of the psychotically depressed and related these feelings to the 'loss of a loved object'. The depressed patient treats *himself* as though he were the lost object. His feelings about himself are also like the feelings of someone who has had disappointment in love. This love, however, is not pure; the patient turns an ambivalent attitude he has had towards a lost person on to himself. On the one hand a pining and a sense of devastating loss is felt; at the same time immense anger burns; the mood is fixed and very dangerous. This is the mood of the suicidal patient, feeling guilt-ridden, worthless, railing against himself. Freud said in *Mourning and Melancholia* that normal grief was the period of time necessary to carry out the testing of reality, to free the ego from the lost object. He remarked how extraordinarily painful this process is, but that this pain seems natural to us. Abraham noted that the loss of a loved person, *or what is felt emotionally as the equivalent of that loss*, could often be found as the precipitating factor in adult manic-depressive illness.[8]

There is substantial evidence that even small children go through states of mind similar to the normal mourning states of adults. But in a review of the effects of bereavement in childhood,[9] Dr John Bowlby described how pathogenic the loss of a mother figure between the ages of six months and six years can be. From six months onwards the infant shows an unmistakable preference for his mother. Until the end of the third year he is very closely attached to her. Long separations during this time can cause obvious, observable distress to the child. After the third birthday, the strength of the child's attachment begins gradually to diminish. A child of, say, fifteen to thirty months who has had a good relationship with his mother shows predictable responses on being separated from her, for example by hospitalization. That is, he will produce phases of *protest*, *despair* and *detachment*, in that order. We are taking an extreme case here where, while the previous attachment to his mother was good, the separation is sudden, fairly lengthy and complete. It is as though the mother had died; indeed, the response in the latter case would be the same. We are describing children who are unvisited and receive relatively unsympathetic care on separation.

Protest will be shown by tears and anger and may last some days. Despair will be shown by his becoming quieter, while hope fades in him that his mother will return. These two phases may alternate with one another, the child being sometimes fretful, sometimes subdued and apathetic. He then seems to reach a point where it is as though he has forgotten her: the phase of detachment. He may appear indifferent to her if she should now come to see him. During all three phases the child is also prone to tantrums and outbreaks of destructive behaviour. Again, we have to note the force of all these feelings. The adult British are notorious for 'hiding their feelings'. This does not mean they have none: children can remind us of the original power of the emotions.

On restoration to his mother, the child may at first be unresponsive to her. If separations have been multiple, or of over six months duration, he may not ever regain his affection for his parents. More usually, 'a storm of feeling' eventually breaks through. From apparent 'detachment' and indifference, the child suddenly expresses the most intense ambivalent feelings towards his mother. At one moment he is clinging and constantly demanding; at another he rages at her, and is angry with her whenever she has to be away, even for a short while. He is highly sensitive to even brief separations from her, easily made acutely anxious by them. The child thus shows what feelings had lain unconsciously behind his apparent detachment. Dr Bowlby comments that the triad – protest, despair and detachment – is characteristic of all forms of mourning. Following bereavement there is always a phase of protest, of trying to recover in feeling terms the lost loved person, as it were angrily reproaching them for their 'going away'. Then there is despair which is also ambivalent, but coloured mostly by pining. Eventually behaviour has to be organized on the assumption of the finality of the loss. This is detachment from the loved object. This triad is a paradigm of *healthy mourning*.

Anger, therefore, is a normal first reaction to loss, however illogical, irrational or futile it may seem to us. It is part of the normal grief response in children or adults. *Pathological mourning* – depression – would seem to be the inability to express or turn outward these feelings; an inability to release, or work through the powerful, futile, but normal, desire to try to regain the loved object and, in particular, to acknowledge aggressive feelings towards it. And unless we can consciously face this part of our mourning response, we will be blocked from going on to the creative stage of mourning, when reparative phantasies reconstruct our feeling lives. In the infancy of a person prone to depressive illness basically destructive feelings were split off and repressed; not enough time was allowed for grieving and, ignoring the true internal feeling situation, the infant went precipitately to detachment. But one cannot disinvent emotions. They go on, and eventually they turn against the self.

Mourning in adults and children thus helps us to understand depression.[10] A number of situations seem able to precipitate a depressive illness. (Experimentalists call this a 'stimulus generalization'.) Adolescence is an unusually vulnerable time for a truly morbid response, as are the puerperium, the menopause and old age, periods when a heightened sensitivity to loss may release abnormal mourning. The adolescent, however, is remarkably efficient in overcoming brief depressions. As time passes this gift is lost. If the early pattern of response to loss – the consciously felt anger – is missed out, this pattern will unconsciously survive, like a computer programme, only needing to be switched on by the right signal – a sense of loss – for the anger against the self to flood back. For example, let us examine the thoughts of a depressed middle-aged woman.

She was obsessed with thoughts of death. Death as an idea frightened, yet fascinated her. At times it was as though all her life had narrowed down until it consisted simply of a wish to die and a restless fear of non-being. She would lie on her bed at night, unable to sleep, afraid to sleep, as though sleep was death; or on some other sleepless night she lay exhausted, fearing to sleep because of the dreams she knew would come. Yet dreams awake or asleep were alike. At best she felt she was in some place where nothing really existed, where she, like the world, had become empty and meaningless. At other times her dead mother would seem to call to her, calling her ungrateful, unloving, urging her to die. Always feeling tired, inadequate and frightened, her past life seemed one vast crime, her present a judgement. She could not eat, because she felt she was too unworthy to be cared for, and because now and then she was convinced her food might be poisoned. At no time did she think herself mentally ill. Life itself had gone wrong.

It is unfortunately impossible to exaggerate the suffering of a psychotically depressed person. In our example of pathological mourning, we can see the high price paid by some of us for living in a guilt culture, and also the dilemma a relative or doctor may find themselves in: that of persuading a dangerously ill person that they are ill. Our example is of a person held in the grip of mourning, pining and guilt; the emptiness of their inner and outer worlds is a result of the loss of the good objects they had set up too precariously in the ego of their infancy.

*

Let us return to the very early situation of childhood, the time of feeding and weaning, when particular patterns of response to loss are established and it is determined whether mourning is to be creative or destructive in the years ahead. The pain of mourning is followed by a reparative drive, an attempt to repair and restore both the inner phantasy and the outer reality. In the depressive position the infant feels that both have been damaged by himself. The pain of mourning and the reparative drives that arise from it are the basis of creativity. In the final analysis it is a narcissistic solution founded on extreme self-love, we might say. The concern for self-preservation is matched, in the reparative drive, by a concern for the apparently lost object and it is from here on that there are possibilities for sublimation – the 'successful renunciation of instinctual aims' – or 'primary instinctual modification'.[11] Here creativity begins.

'Psychotic' mental mechanisms give way to 'neurotic' ones when raw, crude, primitive drives begin to be *inhibited*, *repressed* or *displaced*. Within the exquisitely subtle relationship between a mother and her child, the child begins, ever more definitely, to accept the forms and contents of the culture he has been born into and begins to build up within himself a structuring of his emotions and drives that will, usually, be compatible with this culture. These changes in the nature of mind, apart from the 'physiology of memory' (of which we know very little in physical terms), account for why we remember so little of our early childhood. In Anna Freud's terms, '*instinct has become intellectualized*'.[6] Meanings change and intellectually, at any rate, our own infantile pasts become strangers to us.

Symbol formation inevitably has its origins here. The displacement of a drive from one object to another is the archetype of the use of symbols. The child clutching a favourite piece of blanket or fur shows us a half-way house in forming symbols. This is a 'transitional object', as Dr Winnicott calls it. The grubby bit of blanket stands half way between being the mother herself and the idea of mother safely recreated within the psyche.

The inevitably repeated experiences of loss and recovery, of the mother going and returning, of weaning, but being fed otherwise, of others going and returning, give the child what we can reasonably call repeated experiences of mourning and reparation. It is sound intuition that leads mothers so often to make a ritual of saying 'Bye, bye, see you later.' Even before speech is attained, the child detects the consolatory sound of the words. Loneliness and separation are dangerous in guilt cultures. Teaching the child socialized love and, gradually, how to separate, is perhaps the most important maternal task in the creating of a new individual, out of the multiple possibilities that the mother has borne. Repeated mourning and reparation lead to confidence in the infant in his own ability to love and in his being able to overcome grief. Normal adults mourn, so it is not unreasonable to say that the depressive position of early childhood is never completely worked through. Situations of loss throughout life can precipitate the pain of mourning. Anxiety, ambivalence and guilt at loss reawaken the pattern of earlier depressive experiences.

All being well, mourning, however painful, can be normal and even creative. Creative mourning depends on the love part of ambivalence having been greater than the hate part, for it is this which leads out of the maze into reparation and life. Other animals besides humans can mourn their dead. Perhaps they can be depressed too.

In normal mourning early psychotic anxieties are reactivated. The mourner is, in fact, ill but, because this state of mind is common and seems natural to us, we do not call mourning an illness . . . in mourning the subject goes through a modified and transitory manic-depressive state and overcomes it.[2]

Where hating phantasies seem final and unassailable, mourning miscarries. It becomes destructive and psychotic.

(D) MANIC DEFENCES

There is a condition called a *smiling* depression. The patient may be severely depressed and yet in an interview his features are mobile and he can even smile. Often, while he is busy about his daily tasks, he hardly feels depressed; he hardly feels anything then, he tells you. It is when he has a silent, inactive moment that he may become suddenly *en rapport* with himself and become aware of despair. If he kills himself, the newspapers will say: 'His friends expressed surprise as the victim always seemed so cheerful.' The smiling depression is an example, at a low level of intensity, of *manic defences* at work. It is as though mania and depression were present at the same time. As we know, some famous clowns have had their fun in public and their despair in private. We have discussed how in manic-depressive insanity mania and depression can alternate. In some cases only depressive symptoms are ever shown. Mania can apparently also appear alone. Why should mania be linked to its opposite, depression, at all? Let us answer in the vocabulary we have been using.

The earliest tides of feeling that we can relate to the periodicity of manic-depressive illness are to be found in the alternating feeling states of infancy. We have discussed the extreme ambivalence, the intense levels of love and hate, and the 'oral orientation' of almost all experience at that time. Hunger gathers about it omnipotent anger, screaming and crying, a feeling of being punished; the loneliness of this hunger is felt as annihilation. When fed, on the other hand, the infant feels fulfilled, happy, full of love – and he falls asleep. As he develops, these alternating states of hunger and satiety become connected, in feeling terms, with states of increased and decreased guilt and cycles of pain and pleasure, which establish a kind of expectation that there is a natural order of experience, that the sequel to pain is pleasure, which will be followed again by pain, endlessly; a puritan conscience in miniature. And gradually it is the need for love that takes the place of the need for milk, and the absence of love that can be felt as annihilation. And as the super-ego emerges more clearly as a structure within the ego, it has always an ultimately ambivalent relationship with the ego, half loving, protective, approving; and half punitive and judging. The super-ego, then, is a source of self-love, or self-hate. It becomes a guidance system for behaviour, with a warning function. Small amounts of guilt feelings are warnings, alerting to the risk of greater dangers to the inner world.

Those prone to depression are 'love addicts'.[1] Their self-esteem has been left too dependent on their relations with other people, who must inevitably sometimes seem not to love them enough. The depressed have too much guilt in relation to their own internal objects. Fully developed melancholia, then, brings back the feeling of the complete annihilation of the loved object.

The refusal to eat, so common in depression, springs from the aggressive phantasies of orality, that taking in by the mouth when angry destroys precious things. Feelings of inner emptiness and delusional ideas of poverty all spring from these deeper phantasies of the 'loss of the good object'. Disappointment in love, or any blows to self-esteem are felt in self-love as the same thing. For the vulnerable personality these blows mean not merely the loss of love, but also a loss of existence itself. And the punitive, unrelenting voice of their conscience will only say: this you deserved. The ultimate conflict may be only between phantasies. Yet the phantasies have become 'real' again; they absorb all vitality, narrow down, distort, leave exhausted.

In normal mourning we go through a whole sequence of feelings, and it therefore takes time to carry out what Freud called the 'work of mourning' – the reorientation to one single, giant, final fact of perhaps thousands of separate precious memories of someone.[2] In the process there is a normal regression from an 'object relation' to 'identification' or 'incorporation'. That is to say, a human retreats from the living relationship with the person who has died to having a relationship with an internal representation of him. The funeral feast symbolizes such a shift from 'love' to 'incorporation'; 'sackcloth and ashes' signify an identification with the dead. These paths of normal mourning seem to show that it is easier to 'give up' or detach oneself from introjected objects, than to do so from the real external person. We see here the value of ritual, facilitating these complicated changes in us in which real external relations are replaced by ones only within the personality.

If the mourner had a highly ambivalent relationship with the person he has lost, in the mourning process of incorporating he will, as it were, take in a destructive object. All the hostility he once felt towards the dead person he will now turn on himself. His infantile death wishes towards them rebound on him; he will act as though he has lost his own ego. He will not first feel rage at loss, but guilt. He will act as though he believes his omnipotent destructive phantasies have destroyed the dead person. His self-reproaches originate from the hostility he once felt towards another person. He will feel he can only hate when he tries to love.

We are always, to an extent, ambivalent in our relationships and most of us fear the dead, fearing retaliation from them for those negative feelings we have had besides love; hostile wishes which some part of us feels have, in a way, actually been carried out. Thus we feel some guilt and fear in normal mourning responses. The hypochondriasis of the depressed patient reflects his intenser fear of retaliation, his feeling that he has taken within himself a threatening, devouring, sadistic object; the hypochondriacally depressed often fear they have, for example, cancer, an illness matching in real terms the imagined internal terrors of melancholy.

As these are some of the feelings of the depressed, we have to examine very early phases of infancy to see when they might have arisen, and when normal feelings could go awry and cause severe injuries to 'narcissistic needs', heightened feelings of abandonment or loneliness, and privations in sensitive periods, which will cast long shadows down the years. Perhaps the heredity factor, when it is relevant in affective disorders, operates by making the oral phase of childhood even more perilous and vulnerable than it always is.

Guilt and a great loss of self-esteem are found in depression. In mania there seems to be an increase in self-esteem. The emptiness of the self in depression becomes replaced by an incredibly rich and intensified self in mania, a self 'hungry for objects', full of impulses, where guilt has vanished. In depression, the punitive aspect of the super-ego rules; in mania, the elation seems like a celebration of newly won freedom. But it is also to be seen as the release of the self-love part of conscience; manic egotism is not freedom; rather it is a blind swing in the ambivalent conscience from punishing to praising the ego. In the super-ego of the manic-depressive love and hate are more equally represented. He lacks the belief that his love impulses are more powerful than his hating ones. He is unable to bear his unreasonable guilt. We defined the original 'depressive position' as the time when the infant recognizes a whole object, relates himself to it, and becomes aware of his ambivalence towards it. He fears he has lost his loved object, or is about to lose it. 'When guilt and loss in this situation cannot be borne, the manic defences come into play.'[3] The release of excitement, energy and laughter has been likened to festivals and carnivals when there is a temporary abolition of the restrictions of the rest of the year and the tedium of duty and responsibility can be set aside. It would be foolish for our true temperaments to be judged by our moods on such holidays. Manic patients may feel omnipotent and 'filled again' like a just-fed baby. However, unlike a baby, they cannot now fall asleep easily, but remain difficult, tense and angry, for all their puns, laughter and liveliness. Their laughter itself, infectious though it may be, can be taken as further evidence of the love and hate that cannot come to terms, but see-saw through their lives. There are thus two main defences against depressive anxiety. One is reparation, as we have seen. The other consists of manic defences.

Manic defences have been called anti-analytic, since they try to destroy the basis of reality-testing. They aim at denying the existence of an inner world of feelings, and at denying that it has value. In such denial dependence on a love-object, awareness of loving and hating it, or of feelings of guilt towards it can all be denied. All the highly unpleasant feelings associated with depressive anxiety – feelings of loss, the fear of loss, and pining for the love-object to return – seem to vanish. The 'depressive position' is superficially wiped out. Instead of depression there is mania.

Defence mechanisms used in a much earlier period, but now more highly organized, come into play: denial, in denying dependence; the splitting of objects in the real world and in the inner world; the feeling that things are only good or only bad, widely separated, and not aspects of the same feelingful person within, or out there. Thus, there is no ambivalence, but only idealization – and devaluation. Things are black and white; nothing between, and no helplessness. It is as though the worlds had become extensions of the will; infantile omnipotence has burst out again, with omnipotent control of all reality, and this means, of course, a private reality. A manic patient is for all these reasons difficult to deal with.

Three of their ways of managing their emotions strike one: the first is omnipotent *control*. Nothing is beyond them. Wild, grandiose schemes pour through their heads. Their talk is rapid, excited. Everything is done to excess, with 'flights of ideas'. The opposite from the dependence, the slowing-down and the ruminations of depression. The second interesting feature is triumph. They are elated, sparkling, witty, boisterous, often sexy, even lewd. This contrasts completely with the mood of depressive anxiety. Thirdly, life seems very easy to the manic patient. Nothing is too difficult, or restraining. By devaluing the love-object, by *contempt* for it, the patient can escape feeling guilty towards it. It is not worthy of guilt.

What follows? By attacking the inner, emotional state, by attacking the love-object, which is the source of depressive phantasies, by control, triumph and contempt, depression itself can be denied. The omnipotent phantasies of mania separate the patient from his true, depressed state and for this reason reparative phantasies, which might more truly change the basic emotional pattern, cannot be generated. In mania, underlying depression is not worked through, on the contrary it deepens.

We can now visualize oscillating emotional states, spread over a long time scale, in which a person swings into a depressive illness, suffers for some time and then goes into mania as an escape. (The analogue from cybernetics is 'hunting'.) Neither situation is satisfactory: neither is a solution. Both are riddled with phantasy.

Feelings are infectious. When we say 'How are you?' to someone, they are likely only to reply conventionally, as though it is part of ordinary decency for them to protect us from their true moods. A person answering 'Musn't grumble,' acknowledges this. He will not burden us with his troubles and so we may be grateful to him and like him all the more. If he shows us he is depressed, this might alter our mood. So we collude with one another socially, in denying our true emotional states, by exchanging emotionally neutral noises. In this way we miss helping depressed people.

On the other hand, we fail even to suspect that the mildly manic is odd. We envy him his effortless energy, his wit and drive. We confuse his flight from a basic unhappiness with mental health. We are glad to catch his laughter, and rarely suspect what else is going on inside him.

*

In the infant, however, a solution is found as part of successful maturation. The depressive position is left simply as the likely pattern of emotional response to future emotional loss. The basis of reality-testing is achieved. The omnipotent, loving and hating phantasies are, to a degree, evaluated. Some limits to their effects can be set. A balance between love and hate is struck.

And by his manic defences alternating with reparative phantasies, the infant moves on out of depression, with enough love in him to face whatever comes. Not that this will mean that his future mourning will be without suffering; but it will not be without end. Thus we must modify the paradigm of mourning – protest, despair, detachment – to include the 'passing states of elation which occur between sorrow and distress in normal mourning ...' For the mourner 'goes through a modified and transitory manic-depressive state and overcomes it, thus repeating, though in different circumstances and with different manifestations, the processes which the child normally goes through in his early development'.[4]

5 The Nature of Schizophrenia

What is the nature of schizophrenia? It may seem rather strange to ask this question at this point, when we have already approached the illness in at least three apparently different – yet complementary – ways; once in the chapter on classical psychiatric labels, and again, in quite a different way, in the chapters on early forms of anxiety; the third approach was a brief glance at cultural settings. I ask the question again, because I wish to review in this chapter the main ideas that have been and are still held to be explanatory, ideas that present a complete spectrum of views from organic ones through to others that seem, almost dangerously, to ignore the fact that we have bodies at all. All of these views bring out one or another important point. In discovering what concerns psychiatry, we will find that the attitudes of psychiatrists towards the mad are attitudes that must be advocated for all those who have to deal with the mad, whether as doctor, nurse, relation, friend or by chance confrontation.

It is possible, as we noted in the chapter on Labels, to concentrate on the 'non-understandable' alterations in a schizophrenic personality; from this it is only a short step to suggest that these alterations, as they are not psychological and cannot be understood by the onlooker, have a neurophysiological basis. The label 'process schizophrenia'[1] is given and it is assumed that the puzzling manifestations of psychosis are caused by organic brain disease. However, while a psychotic patient may well have an abnormal neurophysiological condition, this is hypothetical, and we still await unequivocal scientific evidence of it in schizophrenia. In trying to understand psychosis we must be brave enough, mature enough, sometimes to be alone in the dark. We cannot yet entirely explain schizophrenia in causal terms. Unfortunately the importance of emotional factors in the psychotic patient and in his environment has often tended to be dismissed by 'organically oriented' psychiatric specialists. In my section on delirium I hope I shall show that this is a mistaken view even in the unequivocally organic psychoses; in schizophrenia it can also lead to inadequate treatment, as we will see in the consideration of therapeutic communities; it is a mistaken view even if an important physical cause is discovered.

At the other extreme from assuming that 'everything is organic', there is a more contemporary fashion for saying that there are no mental illnesses at all.[2] This can be said brilliantly, but it does not, however, leave the actually mad people in our midst any less mad. Why, we may ask, do those who 'impersonate the roles of helplessness, hopelessness, weakness', whose 'actual roles pertain to frustrations, unhappiness and perplexities, due to interpersonal, social and ethical conflicts', hear voices rather than see visions? Why are they deluded rather than hysterically paralysed? Reclassifying, quarrelling over words, changing the rules of the game, only help when a better theory emerges as a result.

It is only useful to talk of 'multiple factors' in the causation of mental illness if it is made abundantly clear how very different these factors can be in different mental illnesses and in different individuals suffering from the same illness. Thus, many text books state that heredity is an important factor in schizophrenia. Yet 'the great majority of schizophrenics are the children of non-schizophrenic parents'.[3] Many schizophrenics have schizoid personalities prior to their breakdown; many do not – or at any rate, not in the sense 'schizoid' is defined in the texts discussing this point. It is my view that the pre-psychotic personality of a schizophrenic is schizoid in the more complex, less obvious way that I outlined in my section on the 'Origins of Feelings of Persecution'; and that biological, or constitutional factors must contribute in some way. By biological I mean the nature of the organism as a whole – the physical as well as the psychic – and hence we include the constitution in the term and such features as learning ability.

There are four levels on which we can understand mental illness: the *biological*, the *intrapsychic*, the *interpersonal* and the *cultural*. These are interrelated levels of description, each a growing point in our knowledge of madness. The psycho-dynamic infant model with which we chose to characterize and explain psychotic anxieties is a case where one would use a highly subjective descriptive system – one that excludes factors outside the person – i.e. *intrapsychic*. It is almost solipsistic, but the word 'almost' is critical. The 'self' as the only 'knowable, existent thing'[4] characterizes a completely withdrawn, psychotic self. Complete loss of touch with the real world hardly ever happens (except in deep sleep or coma) even though it may seem so to an observer. Our identity as humans, normal, neurotic, or psychotic, partly resides in our being in some kind of relation to other humans, communicating in some way. This leads us to the descriptive level of *interpersonal relations* within a family,[5] or in the world at large. The fourth level is that of *culture:* our general setting, made up of the traditions and values of the community we live in. We have to a large extent learned to be the kind of human beings that we are. To be a man, a woman, or a child means a very different thing in different cultures, or in different sub-groups within a culture; and the evaluation of madness in each culture varies too. Yet we can have an illusory feeling that we have developed and become ourselves from a childhood in which we were striving to unfold and express a basic, single human nature, as though we were fated only to be our unique selves. 'Human nature' is a term which implies a completely common nature. Yet much of our identities as individuals and our assumptions about our rights and obligations as men or women might have been profoundly different if we had grown up in some culture other than our own. We have had to learn much of what is expected of us in terms of behaviour and feelings and only later come to expect these things of ourselves as somehow natural, inevitable and spontaneous.

Biological factors are also relevant. In many cases there seems to be a connexion between physical build and psychosis. An *asthenic* build (slender, with small muscular development) is commoner among schizophrenics than manic depressives. It is associated with longer sojourns in hospital and more severe illness. Schizophrenics with a different physique do exist, but they

are a minority, and are less likely to be severely ill. Heredity
therefore means that in some cases 'genetical causes provide a
potentiality for schizophrenia'. Moreover, human beings are all
one species physically and also, in basic terms, mentally. Despite
our different cultures there are profoundly similar meanings behind our myths,[6] our rituals[7] and dreams.[8] Creation, birth, marriage, death and the forces that oppose us are facts common to
all human experience,[9] and can themselves be at the root of
mental illness: thus the stupor of some catatonic schizophrenics
seems to be a dramatization of the idea of death, and some states
of ecstacy represent the dramatization of being born again.

As the schizophrenic becomes increasingly withdrawn from
reality and as his introversion becomes a disease, he becomes less
and less able to respond appropriately to social situations: his
psychic withdrawal is accompanied by social withdrawal. As he
lets his emotional ties with the outside world drop, so his relationships in it are lost. This makes the psychotherapy of psychosis
very difficult. The relationship between patient and therapist can
at one moment be complex and intense, and then suddenly become infinitely tenuous. Yet all feeling is not destroyed; rather, it
is now turned on to the inner world of the schizophrenic. The self
becomes egocentric again, like an infant, and is able to create its
own answers to its own questions, as though phantasy could
answer real needs.

The withdrawal of emotion from the objects of the outer
world can make it seem dead to the schizophrenic. This is the
origin of the common schizophrenic delusion about the death of
the world, a death which leaves them apparently unmoved. With
all feeling locked away in an autonomous inner world, the
schizophrenic also begins to feel depersonalized. He no longer, or
hardly, exists, in so far as his despair is solitary, unshared, unrelated to other people. From the beginning of infancy there are
anxieties and defences. Reparative phantasies are at first omnipotent. Driven back into infantile ways of ordering inner experiences, the schizophrenic also has phantasies of omnipotent
reparative powers. We say he is deluded if he calls himself 'the
saviour of mankind'. Yet this kind of delusion may be the only
creativity he has left.

The schizophrenic dissociates parts of his ego from himself.

This is an unconscious process, however, and he does not realize that the voices he hears originate within himself. Much that is unconscious in us becomes conscious in him. Yet he does not recognize himself and his own past experiences in his present hallucinations, even though the voices often seem to come from his own head. He has to deny as he projects. He fails to realize that his altered sensations are a result of 'hallucinatory wish-fulfilment', and that his strange sexual experiences, and the altered smells, tastes and feelings in his body all originate from aspects of himself which have become alienated from each other. He peoples his secret world with parts of himself, parts feared, loved or hated. He is the involuntary producer of such terrible inner drama that he can hardly communicate it to us in any ordinary way. His thought disorder breaks up both his and our understanding of what is going on in him. It has been sometimes said that there is a 'glass wall' between us and a schizophrenic. It may seem like this, viewed from the non-psychotic side of the barrier. From his side there is no wall. There is no boundary at all. Our own 'ego identity' is confirmed by our relationships with normal people, but for the schizophrenic both the boundary and the feeling of self are lost. He cannot sort out or understand his experiences because he cannot distinguish himself from the world.

Schizophrenia is an emotional illness, compounded of emotional shocks and conflicts. The schizophrenic's regression to infantile patterns of behaviour suggests that in his early emotional development he experienced certain 'fixations'. As a result of these 'fixations' he reverts to this behaviour whenever strain is too great to continue adult behaviour. Moreover, the infantile-type emotions become greatly intensified because of the greater power of adult feeling. In those cases of acute, explosive, catatonic schizophrenia where recovery is complete, the fixation is entirely purged away during the psychotic period in the violence of what we can call not only reality-testing, but also unreality-testing. Old nightmares are examined in broad daylight and rejected for ever. The patient has enough ego strength to withstand the attack and is only made temporarily abnormal by his inner struggles; he survives because the defences he used in infancy to overcome similar experiences are strong enough to integrate him again. The violence of the illness is an indication of the power of his defences and not only a measure of the virulence of illness itself. That fixations can occur in the earliest period of infancy – the paranoid-schizoid position – suggests that constitutional factors determine a particularly schizoid temperament; for example, some infants are difficult to mother easily, even though they are given love and understanding.[10]

Since the schizophrenic mind has been likened to that of an infant, research has been directed towards the nature of the early relationship between a patient and his mother. Twenty or more years ago the term 'schizophrenogenic mother' had a vogue, particularly in the United States.[11] Such mothers were characterized as covertly rejecting, over-anxious, dominating, frigid and obsessive. The idea that they could cause or precipitate schizophrenia has, however, lost force. More careful consideration of the effect of maternal rejection on an infant shows that it can produce emotional disturbances, but does not specifically cause schizophrenia. And so maternal guilt at having produced a son or daughter who develops schizophrenia is understandable, but unrelated to facts.

Contemporary research has broadened its scope to examine the whole family in which a psychosis appears. Older tests talk of psychotic illness appearing entirely without precipitating factors, but modern studies have found that the family environments of schizophrenics are almost invariably seriously emotionally disturbed. 'Broken homes, unstable parents and an unusual pattern of child-rearing appeared to be almost the rule.'[11] Parents of patients 'seemed to be in chronic discord, perpetually one devaluing the other, with a constant threat of separation'; or 'one parent is dominant and imposes his or her psychopathology on the masochistic partner, who achieves some marital peace by submission. ... The schizophrenic's father tends either to be a passive nonentity, or to sabotage his wife in her role as a mother, being himself motivated by jealousy of a son or by a wish to mould a daughter after his own arbitrary fashion.' The research we are now quoting describes, of course, situations of gross conflict in families; but we are not sure yet that they are specific to schizophrenia. We cannot prove clearly that such families 'cause' schizophrenia. We do not know enough yet about ordinary families and how much conflict they can contain without one or another member breaking down. And yet we can, in our imagination, place the schizophrenic with all his vulnerabilities in such families as these, and think that where we would be unhappy or anxious he might withdraw into madness. For it is in families like these that interpersonal and intrapsychic factors can become equally important. The contradictions and conflicts between persons in the family become summed up and experienced in one single disintegrating mind, the mind of 'the patient'. If neurotic conflicts in families are an important cause of schizophrenia they offer us a new approach to treating the schizophrenic patient. The psychotherapeutic techniques that are so difficult to use with the psychotic may yet help the psychotic patient by being employed in his family, resolving conflict there, where interpersonal relations distort and confuse the roles of the various individuals.

How does the behaviour of the different members of an emotionally disturbed family seem to the member who is called psychotic? To them, he may be seen as 'bad', the person into whom they can project all their own mad or bad feelings in an attempt to feel sane or good themselves. The psychotic person may be caught in a cross-fire of multiple projections of this sort, always being treated by others in the family as a kind of container for their own unacceptable feelings. To the psychotic himself, the other members of the family can appear to constitute an external world matching his internal world, an external population exhibiting examples of behaviour that resemble his inner world of chaotic feelings, which he is desperately trying to make sense of and give meaning to. But there is no rational, coherent outer world for him to check his phantasies against, no common-sense reality to carry out 'reality testing' with. Or, rather, when he anxiously looks out of himself to see if he is only imagining persecution, or conspiracy, he either finds a situation confirming his fears – gestures, or ways of talking, or moving, in the family based on the assumption that he is mad and alien; or else he finds an everlasting ambiguity and denial of reality. Such experiences can either provoke, or augment psychotic anxiety in him. I do not myself believe that such families essentially cause madness, but rather that they release or heighten it in those who are already vulnerable. And, I believe, it is again a question of love and hate going wrong. For the psychotic could only accept the identifications of his family – all their projections – if he believed at some confused level that all these emotional transactions within the family were a kind of loving. Hypothetical as all this may seem, we will later see that readmission to hospital is often greater amongst those patients who have an intense emotional involvement with a key member of their family, the readmissions being at lower rates for those in more neutral emotional surroundings. The human relationships the mad find themselves in are therefore important. We know also, from studies of mental hospitals, that the type of organization of the human environment in the hospital can increase or decrease psychotic symptoms. We shall go into this important fact later in more detail.

In the first chapter I described Billy, an adolescent, standing in a hospital corridor, confused, loving and hating. His mother seemed to be signalling in at least two different ways to him: with anger and with sexuality. He could not deal with either signal; to his internal problems of ambivalence were added an external situation of ambiguity. In the language of labels Billy is psychotic. He has delusions, he hears voices, he giggles inappropriately. One cannot call his mother mad; yet she is involved in his madness. She uses moral terms in describing Billy; he is lazy, stubborn, his own worst enemy, and so on. His strange mental experiences are not mentioned by her, however, though he is willing to talk about them with anyone. We have no reason to suppose that Billy's mother consciously wants her son to be mad (or dead), but the problem of what she wants unconsciously is another matter. What her son means to her can only be worked out in terms of her own childhood, her life history, and her present pattern of living. That her husband deserted her when Billy was small, for example, has meant one thing for Billy and another for his mother's feelings about Billy.

Billy and his mother provide a simple example of a *double bind* situation.[12] The study of small groups of people interacting has led to intense interest in 'communication and information theory' as applied to families. For the patient the double bind consists of a pattern of distorted or ambiguous communication with one or several members of his family. This type of communication is claimed to be the established pattern within the families of schizophrenics.

A neat example of this form of communication is 'the response of a busy mother when her child has fallen and, although unhurt, is crying for comfort. She stops what she is doing and says with great irritation "Oh, come here then." The mother's words tell her child he may come for the comfort he so badly wants, but her tone tells him to stay away.'[13] All children have to learn in growing up which of the two contradictory messages to choose, for this example is very ordinary – such communication goes on between people quite commonly. It is argued, however, that if a child is surrounded by a number of people who continually communicate with him in this manner he may develop a chronic inability to judge which of the two sides of a contradictory communication to respond to. The contradictions in meaning may be conveyed by the voice, as above, or more commonly, by words being at variance with what is being conveyed non-verbally, by posture or gesture, as in our example of Billy. Even if he is crazy, something will not let Billy think of his mother as a sexual object. And as he helplessly notices her erotic non-verbal signals, he has to try to deal with her anger. Eventually, the argument continues, this distorted way of communicating – and there are many complex combinations and permutations of this – leads to a blurring of roles in the family, a confusion of identity, and so to the ego-boundary problems that typify the psychotic. The double bind is like an elaboration of the concept of ambivalence taken over into the pattern of child care. For the victim this 'lifemanship' played for keeps, this creation of no-win situations, can be a potent way of destroying the validity of the feelings that normally guide and adjust behaviour in interpersonal situations. Yet again, little is known about the normal range of communicative behaviour in families, and it is hard to be sure of what is normal. We still do not know whether the double binds found in the families studied are related causally to schizophrenia or not. Yet a whole new approach has been opened up by studies such as these, in that it becomes less and less possible to claim that anyone's madness descends on them 'out of a clear blue sky'.

*

We have conscious memories of the past but we do not classify
our present behaviour in terms of our earlier infantile identities,
unless we are under analysis. We accept ourselves as we seem to
ourselves, here and now. And so we can consider sanity or madness from an existential point of view. It is as hard to believe that
we would have been different as individuals by emerging from
another family, as it is to believe in the unconscious part of ourselves. Yet, and this is especially true for the schizoid temperament, 'Truth and Myth are one and the same thing.' In
Words,[14] the first volume of his autobiography, Jean-Paul Sartre
vividly conveys the here and now of a schizoid childhood. He
does not do it in terms of 'splitting' or 'projection' or 'persecution'. Rather, it is by a series of brilliantly reconstructed situations of a special kind.

I had been convinced that we were born to play-act to each other; I
accepted play-acting but I insisted on taking the lead; yet in times of
crisis, which left me exhausted, I noticed that I had only a bogus 'Solo'
part, with lines and plenty of appearances but no scenes 'of my own';
in a word, that I was supplying the grown-ups with their cues.[15]

It is not merely because Sartre is such a distinguished, exciting
playwright that he characterizes childhood as a series of real or
false roles; he is, after all, also a philosopher.

Our 'being in the world', our existence alone or together,
involves 'playing a part'; not one part, but many. Thus Laing
and Esterson say in their study of the families of schizophrenics[16]:
each person does not occupy a single, definable position in
relation to other members of his or her family. The one person
may be a daughter and a sister, a wife and a mother. They point
out how very differently people behave in their different roles,
how they experience themselves differently, expressing different
attitudes, even quite discordant ones, remembering, imagining
and phantasizing in quite different ways in each role. And it is
arbitrary to regard any one of these alterations of identity as
basic and the others as variations.[17] Laing has commented on the
fact that we expect other people to endorse our own definition
of ourselves.[18] There is a 'wide margin for conflict, error, misconception, in short for a disjunction of one kind or another,
between the person one is in one's own eyes ... and the person

one is in the eyes of the other ... and, conversely, between who or what he is for me and who or what he is for himself; finally, between what one imagines to be his picture of oneself and his attitudes and intentions towards oneself and the picture, attitude and intentions he has in actuality towards oneself and vice versa.'

By exploring identity in this manner, it gradually becomes possible to see a great deal of the behaviour of schizophrenics not just as signs of 'disease', but also as expressive of a mode of existence. The existence of a person with a secure identity follows the themes of *relatedness* and *separateness*, as the person moves from role to role. For *ontologically insecure* people, however, the themes of existence are special kinds of 'existential anxiety', or dread. Every interpersonal relationship threatens insecure individuals with loss of identity. They fear *engulfment* by relationships, even in being understood, loved, or simply seen. In an attempt to preserve their identity they become isolated. Reality itself is seen as a persecutor threatening engulfment. It threatens 'implosion'; they feel the world might crash in and obliterate their identity. The schizoid thus feels both more exposed and more isolated than others do. And besides all the fears that arise from communicating, there is a further fear, that of *petrification*, or *depersonalization*, of becoming inanimate, unrelated, abandoned and dehumanized.

In his 'existential' account of the schizoid condition, Laing gives prominence to a split felt between the body and the self. The true self seems to have become *disembodied*. Bodily experiences and actions are felt as part of a distant, hardly real 'false-self system'; there may seem to be adequate day-to-day gratifications for the body in terms of sex or food; these gratifications may go on, but the real self remains starving, unloved and withering away.

A person becomes more clearly psychotic – schizophrenic rather than schizoid – when, even though the real world is desperately wanted, the false-self system becomes more and more dominant and autonomous, and what 'belongs to it' becomes more and more dead, unreal, false and mechanical. Because of his dread of the effects of a real relationship with another person, he loses more and more the sense of other people's presence; and since ultimately no one else exists, the schizophrenic does not exist either. He has no 'endorsement of his definition of himself', no emotional contact with another person; no one else realizes what it is like to be on the verge of psychosis. He is completely isolated in any community, and even more sharply in a crowd. At this point a person may desperately hurt themselves, or take extraordinary risks in an attempt to feel alive and real again. Up to this point he may have seemed sane to those around him, who have accepted the false mask he has offered them in place of his true 'self'. They are surprised when 'out of the blue' madness emerges. The schizophrenic has killed his 'self' as an ultimate, absurd defence. He has denied 'being', as a strange means of preserving being. Just as once his role was to play at seeming sane, he now as a primitive, magical defence plays at being insane. 'He is dead, in order to remain alive.' He uses complexity, pretence and equivocation to preserve the secrecy of his self, to avoid engulfment, and the threat of understanding. In so doing, he is schizophrenic.

What is there in his family or interpersonal relations that drives him to using such a strategy in order to live? Why does he take such desperate steps? Laing does not claim to explain all schizophrenia, or all schizoid personalities, but he claims that by studying *each person in the family, the relations between them and the family itself as a system*, we can often make schizophrenia 'socially intelligible', and see it as a strategy invented in order to live in an unliveable situation.[16]

A mother describes her daughter Julie's childhood thus: as a baby Julie was perfect, always good, never any bother, easy to toilet train. The comment: existentially the baby was dead. The baby never cried and was never demanding; she was weaned 'without trouble'. She 'adored her mother' as a toddler, and until three or four 'nearly went crazy if her mother was out of sight'. Thus again, psychologically, the child had not begun to become an autonomous person; she had not been emotionally weaned from her mother. Julie was always obedient in one phase of childhood, desperately, in fact obsessionally obedient. Then in her mid teens the girl became 'bad'; she swore; she became untidy; she wandered, and continually ran her mother down. She said her mother never wanted her. This was absurd, said her mother: Julie was her favourite child. Yet Julie said her mother did not want her to become a person. The mother and father, who were sharing a failed marriage, colluded together in accepting only a 'good' daughter. This was a false self for their child. Her real, unique self was always rejected as bad, or denied. It became more and more impossible for the daughter to continue her false role. It was a relief for the mother when her daughter was diagnosed schizophrenic. The mother preferred her daughter's 'bad behaviour' to be explained by madness rather than by badness. The father, on the other hand, never accepted Julie as being ill at all, even though she was deluded, hallucinating and had ideas of reference.

It seemed to me important to give at least a short account of a case which can be referred to in greater detail.[19] The absurdity of schizophrenic symptoms can be seen sometimes then to reflect very curious social settings. And we ask again: which is seed, which is soil?

*

The lack of insight, the denial of emotional needs, the destruction of individual roles in the family, or the creation of false ones, are all descriptions of the family setting of 'the illness'. Only in thinking in a very out-of-date way, namely that humans are completely conscious, rational and free, could we moralize about families containing sickness as these do. We must also be careful not to 'deny the illness' itself: to say there is no psychotic person, but only 'a sick family'. The schizophrenic exists as a person. No human is merely the sum of his interpersonal relations. Yet his interpersonal relations within his family can tell us a great deal about his symptoms. Child psychiatry has no generally accepted scientific classification of children's emotional illnesses as yet; this is both a strength and a weakness. It results from the long tradition of seeing children in a family setting. So many variables are at work that each family emerges as unique. The classical descriptions of adult schizophrenia contrast to a large extent with this situation; they are often descriptions of institutionalized and very regressed patients, and are now only of historical value, acting as a warning against the effects of bad treatment. But to attach technical words to varieties of family transactions and to explain the psychodynamics of a whole family group will not alter the fact that there is usually only one member of the family who is vulnerable and who becomes clearly psychotic. We can perhaps see more clearly, however, why schizophrenia varies so much from patient to patient, in that different family groups introduce so many different factors. We should remember, nevertheless, that biological, intrapsychic and cultural influences also explain schizophrenia.

In this chapter I have tried to examine some of the emotional states of schizophrenics, and to set these individuals, who are products of our culture, into the smaller groups of their families, where feelings first arise and where they can be most strongly felt. I believe that for psychotics the 'environment itself can be the primary treatment as well as supporting or complementing other treatment'.[13] And so we all need much more insight into the insane, since we ourselves form part of this environment.

Part Three

6   From Custodial Care to Therapy – Physical Treatment

Not until 1930* was it possible to be a 'voluntary patient' in a state mental hospital; that is to say, to 'seek asylum'. Even after 1930 most patients in the vast majority of mental hospitals were certified: they were there under legal coercion. This was still the general pattern in the nineteen-forties and -fifties. The hospitals themselves were gigantic buildings, usually situated miles away from the patients' homes, which often made visiting extremely difficult for relatives. The traditions in these mental hospitals were those of a prison rather than of a hospital; the patients were regimented, and the doors to wards kept locked. The main aim was 'custodial care', rather than treatment. There was for the larger part of the day no occupation for the patients and they were ruled over by a rigid hierarchy of nurses and a very few doctors – whose tasks were seen as administrative rather than medical.

The two main objects of custodial care were, firstly, to protect the patient from himself, and secondly, to protect the public from the patient. Of course there were exceptional hospitals – the United Kingdom has made significant historical contributions to the management of mental disorder. Nevertheless, the *average* mental hospital was therapeutically nihilistic until quite late in this century, despite the reforms that were put into effect at the end of the eighteenth century and were extended to one or two asylums in the nineteenth, and to a few more in the twentieth.[1] We have seen that the schizophrenic has severe problems with his personal sense of identity. His thought, emotions and will are disturbed; he suffers delusions and hallucinations. How was he helped by being placed in a ward of seventy or eighty others with

*In Scots law voluntary admission was introduced in 1880.

similarly shattered realities? How did he find his way back when he was cut off from normal life? What did the psychotically depressed person feel when, already guilt-ridden, he was certified and taken behind the walls of a gigantic, barred hospital? Was this not confirmation of the rejection and punishment he felt he deserved? And the senile, already cast adrift from time and place, taken away from their own familiar homes, would give up their last tenuous hold on the world of here and now.

I have devoted a large section of this book to a consideration of how a psychotic communicates with his environment and with himself. It seemed to me this was the most satisfactory way of outlining his handicap. This seemed more useful than giving long lists of incomprehensible symptoms and dozens of potted case histories. The nature of the real world – the environment – continues to be of importance to the insane. A person can be very ill mentally, yet some part of him is still in touch; a 'healthy part' of his ego still remains. But if he has withdrawn either into depression or schizophrenia, he needs more social stimulation, more communication with his environment, not less. And so the effects of depriving people of a normal social life, and of concentrating together just those people who have the most difficulty in communicating with others, can be catastrophic.

*

The scene in progressive mental hospitals has changed beyond recognition. The very term 'custodial care' has now become a term of abuse and condemnatory of the past. In this and subsequent chapters we will examine some of the factors responsible for the change in mental hospitals, a change which has led them to become hospitals in the more usual sense of the word, that is, specialized institutions where sick people receive appropriate treatment. Many modern treatment techniques do not require a patient to enter a mental hospital at all. He may be treatable at home, or, if he does require in-patient care, a general hospital may well have all the facilities required. It is important to realize that psychiatrists themselves differ quite sharply in their attitudes towards different forms of treatment, the *physical*, or the *psychotherapeutic*. This disagreement is unfortunate, but real. A person who is wildly insane is usually too out of touch with reality to be cured by individual psychotherapy, even if there were enough psychotherapists to go round. An intelligent, sensitive person, on the other hand, with a great desire to get well, does not necessarily require physical treatment when only moderately ill, and can sometimes be enriched as a personality by a psychotherapeutic experience.

Professor Fish, speaking of schizophrenia, remarks that many psychiatrists seem to be overwhelmed by a sense of guilt when their patients fail to recover. He points out that psychiatrists, unlike other physicians, are forced to live with their 'failures', who are so often rejected by society and have often therefore to remain in a mental hospital. He contrasts this social rejection of mental patients with the sympathy extended by society to the physically handicapped. Professor Fish believes that out of this 'guilt from a sense of failure' arises the passionate devotion of some psychiatrists to one or other of two main forms of treatment. On the one hand there are the *physical therapists*; on the other, the *psychotherapists*: 'It is impossible to decide which is the most one-sided' point of view.[2] He suggests that the wisest policy is *to use all possible empirical and rational means to help the patient to cope with his illness and its social effects.* I would like to take this view and use it to cover the aims of treatment of all psychoses. Let us first examine the *physical forms of treatment* of psychosis.

*

While in the last few chapters I have been typifying the subjective experiences of patients, in discussing physical forms of treatment I will return to classifying the varieties of psychoses in the way I did in the chapter on Labels. My insistence on the necessity of trying to classify psychoses is based on the fact that a particular diagnosis often determines a particular form of treatment.

The first effective methods of physical treatment for psychosis were discovered in the nineteen-thirties. It could be said that all the dramatic, exciting progress that has been made in psychiatry since then has depended upon these methods alone.[3] What is meant by physical treatment? The term *can* be restricted to cover only 'shock treatments', which we will describe in a moment. However, many psychiatrists regard as physical treatment not only the various shock therapies, but also treatment by drugs and by neurosurgery. The term is taken literally and applied to any physical approach to the treatment of mental disorder. This appears to be a logical view. Let us first explore the possibilities of physical treatment for the *affective disorders* – depressions and mania.

Electro-convulsive therapy, which is sometimes referred to as *E.C.T.* or *electroplexy*, is one of the forms of shock treatment. It originated as a modern form of treatment from the mistaken belief that epileptic convulsions prevented schizophrenia; means of inducing such fits in schizophrenic patients were sought. The idea of producing fits as a form of psychiatric treatment was not new. However, the revival of interest in the relation of fits to psychosis led from methods highly unpleasant for the patient, such as drug-induced fits, to the production of therapeutic fits produced by passing electricity through two electrodes placed on the patient's head. This method was found to be safe and convenient, and by one of those curious accidents in the evolution of ideas, it was found that E.C.T. is dramatically effective not only in schizophrenia but also in endogenous depressive psychosis. Most writers feel compelled, as I do, to explain the origins of E.C.T., so as to show that the original impulse leading to the discovery of the method was essentially a humane one. Psychiatry often saddles itself with provocative names, and 'shock treatment' is such a name. In fact, the method of giving a patient a frank fit, just like that, which has been called 'straight' or 'unmodified' E.C.T., is now very rarely used. The contemporary method is to give *modified E.C.T.* Here, the patient is given an intravenous anaesthetic, commonly thiopentone, so that he is asleep during the actual fit. The fit itself is 'modified' by one or another of an interesting group of drugs, the muscle-relaxants, which briefly paralyse the muscles of the body. The patient therefore is not only asleep during modified convulsive therapy, but he also scarcely convulses. Usually there is no more than a slight twitching of the toes and of the muscles of the face. A number of drugs can relax muscles in this way to modify a fit, but the very short-acting ones are preferred; at present succinylcholine (scoline) is most commonly employed. It is usual to give a course of several 'shocks', each spaced a few days apart.

While E.C.T. is sometimes used to treat the acute symptoms of schizophrenia, it is, as we have said, much more specific in its action in endogenous depression. There is no satisfactory explanation in physical terms of why it is so effective. The depressive illnesses of later life, the *involutional melancholias*, respond best. These patients are the ones who have often been obsessional, rather rigid personalities, and who first break down in middle age. They gradually lose their drive and interests and become incapacitated by their symptoms, which include severe insomnia, hypochondria, intense depression and guilt feelings of a delusional degree; they are more often agitated than retarded. Among this group the patient who tends to early waking with his mood then at its worst, and who shows psychomotor retardation, recovers most swiftly in response to E.C.T.

The 'atypical' depressions, where going to sleep is the problem or where the mood is at its worst in the evening, do not usually do so well with E.C.T.; and, as we might expect, neither does the general group of 'reactive', or 'exogenous' depressions, where other symptoms apart from depressive feelings are prominent – such as anxiety or tension.

The classical manic-depressive psychosis is not magically relieved by electro-convulsive therapy either. It is very important that a doctor should detect the presence of a manic-depressive pattern of illness in the younger depressed patient – that is, under forty. Only when a manic-depressive patient has been depressed for a long time will he be likely to respond to E.C.T. Particularly in people who have a clear pattern of marked swings from periods of mania to periods of depression it will not help. Electrical treatment used in the early part of a depressed phase of manic-depressive psychosis has not only a very transient effect, but may even cause the patient to swing into hypomania which may for a time be even harder to deal with as a medical problem, let alone as a social one. Mania itself was at one time treated by intensive E.C.T., but this approach has fallen into disuse since the advent of effective drug treatments.

Considerable clinical judgement is required in the selection of patients most likely to benefit from electro-convulsive therapy. It is a form of treatment that has aroused passion and prejudice. The fact remains that for a severe endogenous depression where the risk to life from a suicide attempt can be very high, E.C.T. produces the quickest and most predictable improvement, and must have saved tens of thousands of patients from death at their own hands, or from prolonged despair.

We have just mentioned the use of drugs in the treatment of mania. There are various groups of drugs, but the so-called *phenothiazine derivatives*, such as chlorpromazine (largactil), are particularly effective here. Chlorpromazine is in fact a *tranquillizer*, a term used for a large group of drugs which we will consider later in relation to schizophrenia. Under the influence of tranquillizers, the pathologically elated mood and overactivity of most manic patients can be moderated.

But what of the other forms of depression, the ones which do not respond well, or at all, to E.C.T.? Until 1957, E.C.T. was the only effective form of physical treatment for depression, and then, as we have seen, only for some of its forms. In 1957, however, the first effective *anti-depressant* drugs, or *thymo-leptics*, became available to psychiatry. One of these is called iproniazid (marsilid); the other is imipramine (tofranil); they have both given rise to a separate group of drugs, with clearly distinguishable uses.

Iproniazid itself is now generally thought to be too toxic for further use. It was, however, the first *monoamine oxidase inhibitor*, and it was thought to act by preventing the enzyme, or organic catalyst, *monoamine oxidase*, from breaking down serotonin, a compound found in nervous tissues. We need not concern ourselves with the biochemistry of all this, since the levels of serotonin in the brain cannot be linked directly to depression or to the relief of depression. I merely wish to introduce a group of drugs which have an effect on depressive states and which are classified as monoamine oxidase inhibitors – or M.A.O.I. for short. As with E.C.T., there is no satisfactory explanation of how the M.A.O.I. work, but there is evidence enough that they do work.

Iproniazid which fathered the group, as it were, was effective, but sometimes caused liver damage as a toxic effect. The risk of liver damage exists with the later monoamine oxidase inhibitors, but to a lesser degree. Examples of these later drugs are isocarboxazid (marplan), phenelzine (nardil) and tranylcypromine (parnate). These drugs are of most use in *reactive*, or *exogenous* depressions. They take a few days to begin their anti-depressive action, and have a variety of side effects. To typify the group, let us take phenelzine. This drug appears to help patients in whom tension and anxiety are at least as prominent as depression. It also helps the patient with psychosomatic symptoms, whose pains are really masking depressive feelings. As we have said earlier of the people suffering from reactive depressions, these patients tend to have a problem getting off to sleep, rather than with waking early; they tend to blame others for their mood, and not themselves; and the emotional problems they have seem worse to them later in the day than on waking. Often, before becoming depressed, they are particularly well able to cope. *Atypical* depressions, depressions in *young people* and in *hysterical* personalities, can also be helped by the M.A.O.I. Isocarboxazid has been thought rather more helpful than the other drugs in this group in cases with very marked anxiety.

It is important that the patient should receive the right dosage of an M.A.O.I., and that when symptoms are relieved the dosage should be lowered only slowly, or he may relapse. Side effects of the M.A.O.I. group of drugs, apart from toxic effects, only occur infrequently. With phenelzine, they include dryness of the mouth, constipation, and dizziness and giddiness from 'postural hypotension'; impotence, and slight problems in urinating can also occur. One highly unpleasant side effect is a pounding headache. On rare occasions this can be so severe, and associated with so much distress, as well as suggestive physical signs, that a cerebral haemorrhage is suspected. The M.A.O.I. group of drugs all potentiate the action of a large variety of other drugs. This 'potentiation', or increasing of the effect of other drugs, includes increasing the effects of alcohol. They are also incompatible with foods containing tyramine; foods such as cheese or marmite have therefore to be avoided, and alcohol must be taken cautiously by patients on these drugs. Since we are dealing with serious emotional illnesses, the risks from the side effects of these drugs have to be weighed up against the gains achieved when a drug is successful.

The monoamine oxidase inhibitors are on the whole incompatible with the second group, the *imipramine group*. Serious side effects are much more likely to occur if both the M.A.O.I. and an imipramine-type drug are given to the same patient. The M.A.O.I. are also relatively ineffective in the *endogenous* depressions, whereas this type of depression responds very well to the imipramine group; that is to say, the imipramine-type drugs act on the same depressive illnesses as E.C.T. Thus *imipramine* itself (tofranil), and its 'relations', *amitriptyline* (tryptizol), *desipramine* (pertofran) and *nortriptyline* (allegron, aventyl), all have an effect on the depressions we have characterized by symptoms of psychomotor retardation, early morning waking, agitation and excessive guilt feelings. The imipramine group of drugs are somewhat slower to act than the M.A.O.I.; imipramine itself takes at least ten to fourteen days to show its anti-depressant action. The drug can produce unwanted side effects similar to those produced by the M.A.O.I. group. The fact that they are slow to act and are used in the severe endogenous forms of depression where suicide risks are particularly high, obviously indicates that the general management of the patient is still important. Much could happen in the few weeks before the drug begins to take effect. The physical therapist therefore still urges E.C.T. as the first form of treatment for severe endogenous depression, keeping the imipramine-type drug for milder cases. Manic-depressive patients often respond well to imipramine, which is fortunate, considering their poor response to E.C.T. The anti-depressant effect of imipramine builds up gradually, and often the first symptom to improve is the disturbance of sleep; interestingly enough, 'this improvement may be accompanied by vivid dreams, often a good prognostic sign'.[4]

It is usual to increase the dosage of imipramine slowly in order to minimize the side effects and allow the patient to become accustomed to them. As with the M.A.O.I., once symptoms have improved a smaller dosage of anti-depressant is given as a maintenance dose; this may have to be kept up for some weeks or months, and the drug must not be abruptly stopped at the end, but gradually tailed off, to avoid possible re-eruption of symptoms. Manic-depressive patients can safely be kept on a small dose of imipramine for a very long time, and this appears to keep their mood swings under control, the dosage being raised if symptoms become more marked.

One of the effects of the advent of drugs for endogenous

depression has been to reduce the number of patients given E.C.T. Thus a patient who is not severely ill can be given drug treatment in the place of electrical treatment, and those who are thought to need E.C.T. require a smaller number of treatments if they are simultaneously taking the drug. The rather agitated patient can be given a tranquillizer to control his agitation, in addition to receiving his anti-depressant drug, the tranquillizer being dropped when agitation ceases, since tranquillizers themselves sometimes seem to depress.

While the precise mode of action of these two classes of drug, the monoamine oxidase inhibitors, and the imipramine group, remains unknown in terms of their *relevant* biochemical activity, this is not a unique situation in medicine. Doctors use many drugs empirically in all fields. It would of course be very pleasing to know *how* these drugs achieve their effects. Apart from anything else, better drugs with a more swift and powerful action and with fewer side effects, might follow.

It is difficult to separate physical treatment from individual and group psychotherapeutic effects. Nevertheless, this can be done. 'Scientific' results are influenced by what a doctor and his patient *expect* to achieve by drugs and E.C.T. Yet methods have been elaborated for allowing for prejudice and unreal hopes, by 'double blind cross-over trials', a form of elaborately controlled experiment; and we *can* demonstrate the real effect of a whole range of anti-depressant drugs and of E.C.T. upon various forms of affective disorders; we can select the most effective for the particular condition. Many psychiatrists find, however, that unless psychotherapeutic measures are also brought to bear, the essential problem is left unsolved.[5] The life situation is not altered by E.C.T. The basic personality problem is left unchanged. E.C.T. will, in most 'endogenous' cases, shift the present depression. However, unless the human condition changes in other meaningful ways, the depression may return.

Treatment of depressive illness is guided, to a large extent, by the possibility of suicidal attempts. Great skill and judgement are often needed to decide whether or not a patient is at too great a risk to be treated on an out-patient basis. It is very impressive how severe a depression can be contained, however, by a 'therapeutic community' on an out-patient basis. At a centre such as

'Stepping Stones' at Bromley, in Kent, one can see people who a generation ago would have been in a locked ward, but who are now successfully cared for by a combination of voluntary, lay local people and professional people in a club atmosphere. In-patient treatment may be needed where the risks are too high. Even in the old restrictive days mental hospitals had low suicide rates considering their 'high risk' selected populations. The 'open door' policies of modern times have lowered even these.

*

We turn now to the physical forms of treatment for schizo-phrenia. As with the affective psychoses, we will first consider shock treatments before turning to drug treatments. We have already mentioned the fact that E.C.T. is sometimes used to treat acute symptoms of schizophrenia, such as catatonic excitement.[3] However, it is not in any way a specific form of treatment for schizophrenia. The original shock treatment for schizophrenia arose, as E.C.T. did, in the nineteen-thirties. This was *insulin coma treatment*, in which deep states of unconsciousness were induced in patients by the injection of the hormone insulin. This form of treatment has almost entirely died out, being speeded on its way, eventually, by controlled clinical trials to assess its effects, and by the advent of the major tranquillizers. A few senior workers retain a faith in insulin shock therapy, or at least in a modified form, despite the negative results of controlled trials; and some authorities still advocate prefrontal leucotomy, a form of brain surgery at one time thought to be of value in severely disturbed schizophrenics. Most experts now think that tranquillizers have made this procedure unnecessary in schizo-phrenia.[6]

Earlier in this chapter we mentioned the fact that tranquillizers can be used to treat the symptoms of mania and the agitation found in some psychotically depressed patients. A *tranquillizer* is a drug which sedates without making a person sleepy. A great number of drugs have been put on the market as tranquillizers, and exaggerated claims made for them over the last few years. The standard by which new ones are to be judged is that set up by the first really effective one, *chlorpromazine* (largactil). This drug has given rise since the nineteen-fifties to a family of related

drugs, the *phenothiazine derivatives*. They are complex drugs in
their pharmacology, but of interest to us in this context, because
of their calming effect. Excited, destructive or overactive patients
are calmed by them. It follows that they are of great service in
acute schizophrenia where the patient can be wildly excited by
the sudden onset of hallucinations and delusions. However, they
do not only have a calming effect; they also seem to make some
of the apathetic, anergic patients more alert. In some patients the
phenothiazines have the effect of removing all the symptoms of
schizophrenia as long as they continue to take the drug. In others
symptoms are reduced in intensity rather than abolished. These
differing responses again argue against schizophrenia being a
single disease. But at any rate, the major tranquillizers, such as the
phenothiazine derivatives, have vastly improved the outlook for
both acute and chronic schizophrenia, reducing both the acute-
ness of symptoms and, it is believed, the incidence of chronicity.
The point must be made, however, that a certain proportion of
patients, despite all modern forms of physical treatment, do go
on to become chronic schizophrenics. Where their symptoms
are being controlled by a tranquillizer, it has to be accepted
that the drug will have to be taken indefinitely.

The phenothiazines have a large number of side effects, but
these are not on the whole as troublesome as those of the anti-
depressant drugs. A curious rigidity and tremor is common at
high dosage but this can be controlled by other drugs. The other
more minor side effects such as a dry mouth, constipation, or
giddiness, quite often vanish spontaneously as treatment continues. Among the phenothiazines are to be found trifluoperazine
(stelazine), perphenazine (fentazin), thioridazine (melleril) and
several others. It is not at all clear whether one drug is better than
another, but it has been claimed that trifluoperazine is better
than the others in the withdrawn, anergic, rather chronic schizophrenic, and with the paranoid schizophrenic, being more alerting
with the one, and able sometimes to deal with the paranoid delusions and anxiety of the other. For the sake of completeness,
we should mention a newer major tranquillizer, *haloperidol*
(serenace). This is chemically quite unrelated to the phenothiazines, but it has so far received quite good reports as regards
its ability to deal with acute states of agitation and excitement,

and it is therefore helpful in dealing with both acute schizophrenia and mania.

*

The increasingly successful treatment of mental disorders by medication has led to the establishment of psychopharmacology as a subject in its own right.[7] Lithium has now become established as an effective drug for the treatment of both mania and hypo-mania, acting specifically on these excited states, though slowly at first. Lithium also has an important prophylactic action in manic-depressive psychosis, reducing attacks of both mania and depression.[8] Newer drugs acting therapeutically against en-dogenous depressions have joined the imipramine (or 'tricyclic') group. Dibenzepin (noveril), dothiepin (prothiaden), doxepin (sinequan) and iprindole (prondol) have perhaps less troublesome side-effects than older drugs.

Advances have also come in the treatment of schizophrenia. Long-acting phenothiazines, given by injection at one- to four-weekly intervals, have led to remarkable improvements in patients, and can reduce the readmission of patients by over half. [9,10] The dangers of barbiturates as an increasing way of attempting suicide are met by the prescribing of safer hypnotics – for example, nitrozepan (mogadon). Thus chemicals seem to help deal with persecutory[11] or depressive anxiety.

The padded cell, the screams and constant wandering, the wards filled with suicidal patients, outbreaks of sudden violence, all these are of the recent past. Let us see what else helped bring the Hogarthian madhouses of our own lifetime to an end.

The padded cell, the screams and constant wandering, the wards filled with suicidal patients, outbreaks of sudden violence, all these are of the recent past. Let us see what else helped bring the Hogarthian madhouses of our own lifetime to an end.

Social Psychiatry

In this chapter I shall examine, among other things, what is meant by *social therapy*. Social therapy is only part, however, of what is meant by *social psychiatry*, a term which refers to studies of hospital milieu and experiments with therapeutic communities; social psychiatry also covers epidemiological, ecological and cross-cultural research, some aspects of which I have already briefly touched on elsewhere. As we proceed, we will see that, just as physical treatment need not be given only to patients inside mental hospitals, but can be made available to out-patients also, so much of social therapy can also be given on an out-patient basis. The population studies included in the scope of epidemiology can often guide us to the most profitable ways of offering help to the mentally ill, helping us to provide the kind of treatment facility which is most beneficial in different cases. We are mainly concerned with schizophrenia and the depressive disorders here, leaving the senile psychoses to a later chapter.

There has been a revolution in psychiatric practice and the evidence of this is to be found in the increasingly shorter periods that patients spend in mental hospitals, even if readmissions have simultaneously gone up.[1] In the previous chapter we saw that effective physical forms of treatment have emerged only in recent years, and that these forms of treatment came in when in many mental hospitals nothing that could be called medical treatment had been offered previously. We also remarked on 'exceptional' hospitals of the recent and remote past, implying that there were ways of treating psychosis that hospitals that were only offering custodial care had ignored. This treatment is nowadays called *social therapy*. But before we attempt to describe what is meant by therapy, let us first sketch out the changing scene.

The most important themes in contemporary British psychiatry arise from the changes in social attitudes towards mental illness, changes both in psychiatry itself and in the community at large. While still more change is required, and it would be foolish to ignore various obstacles to understanding, a fresh wind blows. We can say now of the institutions required to offer psychiatric treatment:

... the evolution of social organizations can no longer be said to proceed by change ... planning, control, and social design are becoming ever more prominent. This trend ... leads to a whole intensity of awareness of the urgent need for better understanding of social organizations of all kinds.[2]

As a reflection of this trend, a new Mental Health Act was passed in 1959. The idea behind it was that psychiatric patients should be able to seek treatment with no more formality than for any other type of illness. The aim was to end destructive 'custodial care'. Let there be no misunderstanding of the revolutionary implications of this Act. It led to thousands of 'decertifications' of patients then in hospital, and promises to lead eventually to a very much higher standard of treatment of psychiatric patients. Another important part of the Act was to make it possible for any type of hospital with suitable facilities to accept psychiatric patients. Special hospitals were no longer to be 'designated' as mental hospitals. An obligation was laid on local authorities to provide community care. Compulsory admission powers were also altered but retained. Obviously *some* compulsory powers are sometimes necessary, since psychotics often lack insight into their illness, particularly into the fact that they *are* ill. None of us, doctor or layman, would care to stand by having 'responsibility without power', while an actively suicidal person, for example, went on refusing help, denying that he was ill. Such a patient can look back with wonder at a half-forgotten memory of how ill he was; he can often have insight in retrospect. He can accept that someone else, in a very temporary parental role as it were, had to take responsibility for him for a little while. But this must be for a *little* while, and in a medical setting: he must not be held in impersonal custody, untreated for years, powerless to alter his situation. Most patients are now admitted as 'informal' patients; a minority need compulsory admission, but of these most become 'informal' patients within three days or a month. A new act of parliament was hardly needed in a number of progressive mental hospitals, but it was overdue for the rest. Some of the leading hospitals are listed in Enid Mills's book, *Living with Mental Illness*.[3]

What were the elements that permitted social change? An act of parliament? It could hardly do more than permit to happen what could already happen. The influence of psychoanalysis must be acknowledged. The influence of Freud spread far beyond psychiatry. History, art, literature, anthropology, criticism, films, philosophy, even music, have changed because of him; even cartoonists should be grateful. And all these aspects can be considered as a 'public relations' job, narrowing the gap between 'them' and 'us'. 'None of us is normal' has come into our language; we have all become a little 'analytic'. Yet ironically enough, Freud did not believe that psychoanalysis could be used to treat a psychotic individual. Indeed, the main difference between British and American psychiatry, for example, lies in the development in this country of social therapy for groups of psychotic patients, whereas in the U.S.A. the stress is largely on psychodynamic psychiatry applied to individual neurotic patients. Yet the lay image of a psychiatrist in this country is still largely that of one treating an individual patient, and the difference between neurosis and psychosis is still largely misunderstood. Of course individual psychotherapy of neurotic patients does take place in the U.K., but as far as psychosis is concerned it is not usual practice. A tiny number of psychotic patients have individual psychotherapy. This is a very rare and, to an extent, experimental approach.

At any rate, psychodynamic ideas have made madness itself understandable. In addition, physical forms of treatment have emerged; they not only treat mental illness, but in themselves reduce public anxiety about madness, by indicating that the mad can at last be treated, controlled, or made more 'predictable', and so need not be merely treated by 'denial, isolation and insulation'. Numerous other elements have come in. It is felt that people are less explosively mad now than they were. This leads, of course, to more tolerance by the community. Thus the new Act was accompanied, to some extent, by a readiness on the part of the public to accept its implications. There has been a kind of vast interaction between the general community and mental hospitals, for just as the community at large can now bear many more disturbed people in its midst, so some of the features of normal communal life have come into hospitals.

Together, physical treatment and social therapy suddenly produced in the middle nineteen-fifties a totally new medical situation. *For the first time since records had been kept, the numbers of patients in mental hospitals began to fall.* Some of the old custodial asylums became *therapeutic communities*, and the level of public tolerance of psychotic symptoms rose sufficiently for it to be possible for patients who were still fairly ill to leave hospital, or not to go into a mental hospital at all. The fall in patients admitted to hospitals was so sharp that it was calculated that the number of chronically mentally ill people needing accommodation would be halved over the next fifteen years. It was partly because of this trend that the 1959 Mental Health Act was justified; and the section of the 'Ten Year Hospital Plan'[4] dealing with future psychiatric needs in the U.K. is almost entirely based upon it. The Mental Health Act was also a new attempt to correct and bring up to date older legislation that hampered efforts to treat patients early in their illness, and to allow newer methods of treatment to be brought more freely into action. The Act can also be seen as an attempt to remedy a fantastic division in medicine itself, involving a dual morality in which physical illness had been receiving almost all the respect, sympathy and financial support of the Health Service, while mental patients, occupying half the beds provided by that service, were the poor relations of the physically ill in almost every sense.

We must, however, put in a few words of caution. The first is that as plans unfold for the community care of patients outside hospitals, the mental hospital may become a repository for the least treatable. This concentration of the very, very ill will be bad for them and a thankless task for the staff who care for them. We must not 'idealize' our new techniques and in doing so blind ourselves to the fact that a number of patients still, despite them, become chronic invalids. Better results *have* been obtained in hospitals and other communities we have devised. These 'sub-cultures' of the mentally ill, once isolated, are now related more and more to the general community. But they continue to contrast with it, and this is, in itself, a problem. Public attitudes towards the mentally handicapped remain vitally important. It has been suggested that we will eventually not need mental hospitals at all. Let us hope this is true. It will not be true in any real sense if patients are simply discharged from hospital still unwell and with no adequate after-care. Again, it is not necessarily a good thing that the psychiatric beds attached to general hospitals are going up from 5,000 to 9,000 under the Ten Year Hospital Plan. Therapeutic communities have mostly developed peripherally, away from academic centres. Bad geography becomes good therapy. Doctors who have not cast themselves in the traditional roles of 'proper doctors' are able to see disordered behaviour in social terms, while those with the biases of neurology and organic medicine continue to search for 'disease entities' in individual patients. An annotation which is in a way a comment on this latter view calls itself *Blurred Signposts in Schizophrenia*.[5] It reviews some of the mass of negative findings of somatic research on the illness. A great deal therefore depends on community techniques – on social therapy; psychiatric units in general hospitals must provide this therapy if they are to help, and not be merely 'ivory towers housing a *corps d'élite* of patients and staff'. Furthermore, these units must be comprehensive and fully integrated with the rest of the psychiatric services.

The Ten Year Hospital Plan outlines official estimates of future hospital needs as far as the nineteen-seventies. Its view of the psychiatric services is, as we have said, that fewer and fewer hospital beds for mental patients will be needed. The plan has been quite severely criticized.[6] For example, it takes no notice of regional variations in the pattern of mental illnesses. Its calculations are based on an unusual period – the nineteen-fifties – when 'institutionalism' was more widely discovered and began to be combated. This was not always so much purely psychiatric progress as institutional progress. Officialdom looks to community services to substitute for hospitalization rather than to complement it. 'The statisticians have measured usage, which has innumerable determinants; the planners appear to have assumed, with no evident justification, that this may be taken as a measure of need.'[6]

A more recent survey of a particular region divides opinions into the 'optimists who ... believe that new drugs and community-care policies can halve the mental hospital population and the pessimists who believe that the psychotropic drugs are merely palliative and the local authorities less than enthusiastic about community care'.[7] This latter well-organized study has the title *Too Few Psychiatric Beds*. I believe it makes its point. Officialdom appears too eager to believe half the problem is solving itself.

Since hospitalization on a fairly large scale will continue to be necessary for the more extreme psychotics, I will write in some detail about the new specialized therapeutic communities. An understanding of these communities adds to an understanding of madness. As we learn more about social change in these settings, so social therapy will become more effective. The Registrar General's figures of 1964 shows that in ten years there has been an increased 'first-admission rate' for manic-depressive and senile psychosis; the rate for schizophrenia has remained mainly static. There are, then, large numbers of patients falling ill and needing some form of treatment. Community services are growing and hostel accommodation, for example, provided by local authorities, rose from 115,000 in 1960 to 140,000 in 1963. There is, therefore, a very strong move against putting psychotic patients into mental hospitals where they are out of contact with the general community. Special arrangements are also being made for patients leaving hospital who still need care and either have no home to return to or are unable to return home.

*

Let us now compare old custodial care with therapeutic care. We are not as a society very accustomed to the symptoms of psychosis. For many years psychotics have been hidden away in remote asylums. They have been skeletons in the dark cupboard of society. In studies of simple societies where our kind of alienation has never taken place it is still possible to identify people who are experiencing a major psychosis recognizably similar in its symptoms to those of psychotics here in the United Kingdom. But in these so-called primitive communities only a minority of psychotic illnesses become chronic, and very few of those chronically psychotic deteriorate severely. That is, most of these psychotics, even those chronically disturbed, are still partially able to adjust to normal society.[8] This contrasts strikingly with what used to happen in the United Kingdom, where chronic psychosis was often accompanied by social deterioration, and suggests that our custodial methods of dealing with the insane were more destructive than doing nothing at all.

The very concept of mental health is a difficult one to grasp. The usual objection is that mental health has to be defined with reference either to criteria set up by the psychiatrist himself – and psychiatrists vary greatly in their approaches – or to social norms. Both methods lack objectivity. In an earlier chapter I dealt with the problems of cultural relativity. For decades psychotic deviation led to swift certification. We now think we can treat medically what was previously more a matter of legal 'disposal'. Under the old Lunacy Acts the law established various criteria for action; it seems to most of us that contemporary psychiatry is far less arbitrary in its criteria. *It is often by being non-moralistic and informal in dealing with psychotics that we can be most helpful.* If a neurotic patient can feel that his therapist does not pass judgement on him he will ultimately be able to face the least acceptable part of himself. The passive acceptance of the weakness of the psychotic ego enables a psychiatrist to work with the healthy part of the patient. These non-judging attitudes should not be only a characteristic of psychiatry; they should be adopted by the general community as well. The psychotic notices this kind of acceptance gratefully; beyond all subtle arguments, we are concerned with the necessity of doing practical things.

Quite simple measures can have dramatic effects. In a particular traditional hospital in the nineteen-fifties I ran a 'therapeutic group' of chronic schizophrenic women. They were not used to being in a 'personalized' group, nor were they used to this kind of relationship with their ward doctor. Their former contact with him had been in the form of brief interviews at various intervals, as was laid down by law, in which their psychotic symptoms were sought and noted down – their weaknesses rather than their strengths. They lived in a locked ward and were cut off from the outside world, not merely by their symptoms but also by their environment. They were almost totally unoccupied and un-productive. The greatest safety seemed to lie in silence. Yet, as one sat silently with them, one felt that somehow a great deal was going on. For one thing, a number of normally very restless patients were able to sit fairly still for an hour. There were small movements of non-verbal communication: inclinations of the head, small gestures from one patient to another. A psychopath joined the group without invitation one day. She spent the first half hour verbally attacking the doctor. 'You can't de-certify me, can you' – angry, bitter, 'castrating' words, mostly true. Yet this attack provoked several of the schizophrenic patients to come to the doctor's rescue and defend him. He was 'trying to help'; it 'was not his fault'. Two patients spoke who had been mute for months. And what they said made sense.

*

Dr Maxwell Jones was the pioneer of the therapeutic community proper – 'a small face-to-face intensive treatment facility with extensive social restructuring'.* This approach remains, however, an unusual form of treatment. Few mental hospitals can yet offer such a sophisticated and complex form of social therapy, and only a minority of psychiatrists working in mental hospitals are capable of giving it. The more familiar and increasingly widespread form of 'therapeutic community' operates at a more general level. It nevertheless constitutes an enormous advance in the management of psychosis as compared with former techniques.

The 'Worthing Experiment' was a pathfinder in the nineteen-fifties.[9] By energetically applying all available psychiatric tech-niques – visiting patients in their homes, building up out-patient facilities and organizing social services for patients – the problem of increasing overcrowding of the local hospital wards was not only dramatically solved, but the quality of the psychiatric care given to patients, who often no longer needed to be admitted to hospital, was also raised.

One of the major drives behind the recent spread of treatment and care for psychotics as distinct from mere custody was the re-

---

*To be accurate, therapeutic communities were originated in the 1942–3 'Northfield Experiment', before Maxwell Jones evolved his ideas. (Maxwell Jones, *Social Psychiatry*, Tavistock: Routledge, 1952.)

discovery of the importance of environment for patients. With this rediscovery came the realization that the conditions in many mental hospitals practising 'therapeutic nihilism' meant that patients not only received no treatment, but also that their symptoms actually increased. It became an urgent problem to prevent patients going into such environments, unless the social and medical crisis they were undergoing made no alternative possible. Much of the development of psychiatric services outside mental hospitals is a result of this. Another task was the re-examining of the structure and function of the hospitals themselves.

Christopher Caudwell objected to psychoanalysis[10] because it seemed to him to claim a monopoly of the truth about society and to imply that the only alternatives in life were to adapt to conditions or to perish. Indeed, these were the two alternatives in many mental hospitals, in an emotional sense, and there is this aspect of psychotherapy in second-rate hands: the patient is wrong: the psychiatrist, the nurse, the hospital, society, are right. Caudwell was right to insist on the weakness of a view that ignores the actual conditions under which a person exists, even though the concepts used in psychoanalysis may be applied to social situations. His maxim, 'We must change the world in order to change ourselves', may sound like adolescent idealism. Yet in some ways he is very right: we must change an inert hospital environment, we must respect the personal value of each patient, we must create conditions for hope.

The history of madness has been inevitably bound up with problems of religion and of the law. In remoter times the symptoms of psychosis were seen as proof of the existence of witchcraft. Those we now call psychotic were once treated with incredible cruelty in an attempt to drive the devil out of the body which, it was then thought, could be possessed by an evil spirit. We can see how the paranoid schizophrenic would confess to being possessed, as voices alien and hostile called to him; or how a depressed old woman, suffering from delusions of guilt and worthlessness, would admit to practising witchcraft, or anything else that seemed to her to epitomize the worst crime of her era. In later times, the law became concerned with the fate of mental patients: those whose illness prevented them looking after themselves or their property, and who might harm other people or themselves. Early legislation was impressively enlightened and humanitarian, and was matched at about the same time – the middle of the nineteenth century – by reforms in the running of asylums, such as systems of 'no restraint'. Previous forms of physical treatment, purging and bleeding and the use of strait-jackets, were brought into disrepute. Patients were found to improve as a result of increased freedom and, in some hospitals, were even given treatment aimed at rehabilitation.

Unfortunately the 'Lunacy (Consolidation) Act' of 1890 had very destructive effects. This act was passed as a result of public concern about the risk of improper detention in asylums. In an attempt to prevent wrongful detention it laid down that asylums would only receive the certified, those patients who were obviously very mad. This meant that no more attempts were made to provide early treatment and that easy discharge was at an end. Another result of this legislation was that all seriously ill patients were gathered together, so that asylums grew from the manageable to the monumental. Thus, while in 1850 twenty-four asylums had each an average of 300 patients, by 1900 seventy-seven asylums had each an average of 1,000. Having lost their early treatment and early discharge functions, asylums became gigantic prisons for the insane containing hundreds of terribly ill patients, physically restrained and cut off from the community as effectively as their symptoms cut them off from each other. The Maudsley Hospital was one of those that attempted to break away from the 'strait-jacket' of the law by being an 'undesignated' hospital, that is, patients could be admitted without being certified. Opened in 1923, it was endowed by Dr Henry Maudsley with the specific aims of providing early treatment for acute psychiatric cases, out-patient facilities, and a centre for research and teaching. However, the general picture in the U.K. hardly changed until the new approaches to treatment we are discussing developed, and the 1959 Act was passed, with its emphasis on therapeutic communities.

It could be said that contemporary forms of physical treatment are completely responsible for the freedom that is now allowed to the psychotic. However, the question is not so straightforward. In certain hospitals various symptoms of psychosis declined or disappeared *before the advent of the newer physical treatments,* for example the so-called 'chronic catatonic features' to be found in older texts – 'regressive incontinence', 'autism', 'flexibilitas cerea' (a curious waxy flexibility of the limbs).

Some of the most striking symptoms of psychosis were actually produced by the old asylums. In a brilliant book on psychosis, one of the earliest attempts to present a psychodynamic account of psychoses (which is still in print), there is a curious passage, a comment on how easy it was until very recently to make mistakes over apparently 'classical' symptoms of psychosis. Here apathy is erroneously treated as a psychotic symptom: 'In ... *apathy* the patient is neither excited nor depressed but absolutely indifferent and without apparent interests, desires or ambitions ... best exemplified in the so-called *emotional dementia* which characterizes many of the chronic patients who constitute the permanent population of the hospital'![11]

The author goes on to describe ' expressionless faces and hanging heads' and shows how 'dementia' (loss of mental powers) is more apparent than real. We would now call this the result of *institutionalization*. This kind of apathy is not part of psychotic illness, but the effect of a deadening environment. It is what Russell Barton calls *Institutional Neurosis*,[12] an illness added to illness by the way the sick are treated. People become objects, because they are treated as objects, stripped of individuality and personal value. Barton describes institutional neurosis as a 'loss of interest, especially in things of an impersonal nature, submissiveness, apparent inability to make plans for the future, lack of individuality and sometimes a characteristic posture and gait.' Writing in 1959 he said of schizophrenia: 'Thus, after four years in mental hospitals, most patients are suffering from two illnesses (1) Schizophrenia, (2) Institutional Neurosis.' He noted that the neurosis occurs in other institutions apart from mental hospitals, in prisons, orphanages and so on. He also noted that rehabilitation resolves its symptoms and that hospitals run by a staff aware of the risk of such a neurosis cease to produce it. A bad institution therefore has two effects: *patients may be made madder and they may acquire a neurosis*.

The first general assault on apathy and therapeutic nihilism in the mental hospitals of the twentieth century did in fact come from the rise of the new physical forms of treatment. We need not go into detail about much of the early treatment as it has been superseded by newer methods, and was of limited therapeutic value in itself. But the impact on the morale of mental hospital staff was decisive. Through insulin shock treatment, E.C.T., and prefrontal leucotomy, staff could at last feel that their task was to treat patients rather than merely to observe and restrain them, and patients actually seemed to recover as a result of these treatments.

In the course of time we have come to realize that though insulin shock treatment, for example, is a mythological form of treatment in itself, which does not survive scientific evaluation, patients improved because they were selected for it, and not by magic, or by mere suggestion. Of the patients selected for treatment, some were just the ones who would have done best anyway. But apart from this, they were formed into a small group with better general conditions than the rest of the patients, who were living in hopeless, institutional squalor. The selected group received the best medical and nursing care, and lived in an atmosphere of optimism because of the prevailing faith in the form of treatment. When insulin was discredited as a treatment, the benefits of grouping patients together, occupied, and under conditions of high staff morale and reasonable therapeutic hope, became in themselves lessons that had been learned, at least in some hospitals. Gifted heads of hospitals were intrigued by the effects of what was coming to be seen as social therapy. As the newer and more truly effective physical treatments emerged, 'total push' programmes were devised, in which rehabilitation, art therapy, work therapy – even music therapy – were tried, combined with physical treatments.* Occupational therapy was rediscovered as a physical form of treatment. For example, patients who had received prefrontal leucotomy made much better progress if they were given intensive occupational therapy afterwards. Many psychiatrists feel that this situation was identical to that found with insulin, and that it was the interest taken in the patients by the occupational therapists that counted, rather than the treatment itself.

*There had long been evidence of its value, e.g. Hermann Simon, 1927, M.P.A. special publication, 1930. This earlier evidence had been generally ignored.

Perhaps the most important change in mental hospitals was the so-called 'open door' policy. We have called the late nineteenth- and early twentieth-century hospital a prison for the insane. At a few hospitals – Dingleton Hospital, Melrose, Mapperley Hospital and Warlingham Park – it was shown that locked doors were not only an affront to human dignity, but that an open hospital could actually function better. With adequate treatment and planned activities and amusements for patients disturbed behaviour lessened. Many of the old problems in locked wards came to be seen as the responses of psychotic people to boredom and frustration. The drama of increased psychotic symptoms was a reaction to conditions which would be intolerable to any human being, even though the types of anxiety and behaviour displayed could not be explained by the situation itself, which is why we dealt with psychotic anxieties in a separate section of this book.

And so the progressive mental hospital of the nineteen-fifties had all or almost all its ward doors open. Patients no longer became institutionalized by idleness, or made madder by being imprisoned and thus denied their self-identity and personal needs. Programmes of occupation were planned, and these have become more and more realistic as forms of industrial therapy, rehabilitating the patient by recognizing that he hopes and is eventually expected to leave the hospital and must then earn his living. The National Health Service also brought new funds and an improvement in the status of psychiatrists. The physician superintendent, the head of the mental hospital, was no longer encouraged to run his hospital in an authoritarian, strictly hierarchical way, for it became gradually obvious that this was an anti-therapeutic form of management, crushing endeavour and discouraging change.

And so we can see how the nineteen-fifties, a time of change and great improvement in the treatment and management of patients, and a time of new enthusiasms, produced a striking alteration in the trends of admission and discharge of patients: at last the numbers of patients kept in hospital began to fall.

Few manic-depressive or depressed patients presented the problems of extreme chronicity shown by the schizophrenic, even before modern treatments were available. The numbers are

still smaller now. At one time it was hoped that the new methods
of management and treatment would solve the problem of the
schizophrenic patient becoming a chronic invalid. These hopes
have not been entirely fulfilled. A significant number of schizophrenics go on to be chronically ill, that is, for longer than two
years. Nevertheless, the therapeutic community we have discussed, one in which patients are occupied in small groups,
treated with tranquillizers, and regarded as human beings,
prevents chronic patients from acquiring an institutional neurosis,
or becoming madder. The social effects of their illness are thus
minimized. These methods of occupational and social therapy,
combined with physical forms of treatment, constitute the most
widespread form of treatment in the U.K., whether they are
employed within hospitals or, as contemporary legislation and
attitudes permit, outside them.

Social therapy on an in-patient or out-patient basis means
organizing groups of patients and personalizing the relations
between members of the group, which includes medical or nursing
staff. The groups must be more organized than neurotic groups
need be, since psychotic patients are obviously far less able to
manage their social lives. The old segregation of the sexes has
ended and this has also led to behavioural improvement. The
whole theme of social therapy affects the staff in the situations
where it goes on; with the previous hierarchical staff structure
all communications and directions came down a chain of command, and the final recipient, the patient, often had no one to
communicate to. Now, with the impact of a more democratic
system in hospitals, there is much freer communication between
patients and staff, and between the staff themselves. Only in a
personalized situation with maximum psychological contact
between the patient and his human environment can the patient's
emotional needs really be known. Staff meetings involving nurses
and auxiliaries, and doctors, are regularly organized in order to
facilitate this contact, so that a constant reassessment of the
patients' capabilities can be made; and also so that his social
rehabilitation can be continuously, appropriately and flexibly
rearranged. And so it is that a day hospital or a mental hospital
can be a busy, friendly place, where all the contacts a patient
makes are evaluated in terms of their therapeutic effects – contact

with nurses, with occupational therapists, in a patient's social club, at music or art therapy. The patient is given responsibility, as soon as he is well enough to take it, in organizing some social activity and in the kind of work he is offered. A series of intermediate facilities can be offered as the patient improves. Outpatient departments and day hospitals help the patient towards more complete social functioning. He may, for example, go out from the treatment centre to sheltered or ordinary work; or he may live in a special hostel rather than return home. The keynote of modern treatment is flexibility and continued social support where necessary. The social consequences of illness are thus minimized and, in addition, the intensity of the psychotic illness itself is reduced.

A totally neglected aspect of madness has been the loss of self-confidence and the pervading sense of personal and social failure which may remain even after the tumultuous symptoms of madness have died away. Some of this feeling may be due to a legacy of doubt about oneself. One has had to face emotional experiences and aspects of oneself that are difficult to accept. Indeed, the way we are made and brought up seems designed to prevent us from seeing that we are both 'more moral and less moral than we think we are'. In an 'anti-alienating' community great loss of confidence as a result of social rejection is, to a very large extent, preventable.

*

Earlier in this chapter we mentioned the 'therapeutic community proper', a 'small face-to-face intensive treatment facility with extensive social restructuring'. A small number of workers claim a good response on the part of psychotic patients to this sort of régime.[13] This is important as there is still a problem of chronicity in psychosis, particularly in schizophrenia, and we cannot yet rest content with present techniques. The original form of therapeutic community of recent times had an immense influence on the thinking of psychiatrists, even of those who did not copy it exactly, but went on to organize the kind of communities we have just discussed. The therapeutic community incorporates a method of elaborate *interpretative* group psychotherapy in a planned community. It has therefore many of the features of the communities already outlined, but abnormal behaviour is also interpreted;

that is to say, a general view of the mind is required, a psychoanalytic model, which can be brought to bear in attempts to understand behaviour. Few psychiatrists are highly trained enough to carry out this work, because the majority of psychiatrists in the U.K. are eclectic rather than psychoanalytic. We have attempted to convey a view of mind derived mainly from psychoanalytic thinking that can be used to understand psychotic experience and behaviour. But we have said, in discussing modern, progressive hospitals, that the behaviour of the whole community, staff as well as patients, has to be examined and understood. This means that in a community that interprets behaviour psychoanalysis has to be applied to the non-psychotic as well as the psychotic. In an earlier chapter we picked out the differences between the so-called normal person, the neurotic, and the psychotic. The difference between the neurotic and the 'normal' is more one of degree than of kind. It is beyond our brief to give even an outline of those aspects of psychoanalysis that are applicable to non-psychotic situations, but we can point to a few of the features that have influenced the design of therapeutic communities. Firstly, the basic psychodynamic view that much of our behaviour, neurotic or normal, is influenced by unconscious processes in us. An inflexible view of causality is applied to human behaviour here; every behavioural event has an antecedent cause, if we could but identify it. The view that there 'must be cause' for our behaviour leads to the analysis of behaviour. People are not simply neurotic, normal or mad, but are perhaps reacting with different means at their disposal to various events around them. The Oedipal situation is applied to the social situation: sons may fear, love and hate strong father-figures, whom they unconsciously feel to be rivals for the love of mother-figures. The development of therapeutic communities has therefore led to a reassessment of the role of the physician superintendent, the omnipotent father-figure of but a few years ago, and of the kind of figures – male or female – who can generate the wrong kind of emotion in staff or patients.

One of the landmarks in the literature of the evolution of mental hospitals is the study called *The Mental Hospital* by Stanton and Schwartz.[14] This work, which incorporates 'a three year socio-psychiatric study of a ward in a psychiatric hospital', brings out clearly how the *traditional* roles of therapist, hospital administrator and nurse can be in profound conflict. Their individual behaviour may, in fact, be derived from their own personal needs rather than from the needs of the patients.

A critically important point, made very clearly in *The Mental Hospital*, is how *destructive traditional 'labelling' can be*. For example, a young, female 'catatonic schizophrenic' was frequently described in ward reports in psychiatric jargon – she was simply 'disoriented', or speaking in 'word salads', and so on. Eventually, almost by chance, it was discovered that the patient was worried about where her personal clothes had gone; they had in fact merely been stored. Because of her incoherence, it was not easy to find out this simple fact. Yet, on it being carefully explained to her where they were, her overactivity and incoherence gradually ceased. There are many examples in this and other studies of how the meaning behind incidents in human groups can be discovered, if only the situation in which they happen can be adequately analysed. This can lead, of course, to the avoidance of provocative acts or aggressive outbursts and to a general reduction in symptoms – apart from a decrease in the use of jargon. Lessons like this can equally well be applied to situations outside hospital, wherever an ill person is.

An analysis of a situation in sociological terms means taking account of all those present, staff and patients. There must be a pooling of intellectual skills and emotional resources. An essential question is 'to what extent do hospitals impede or facilitate the recovery of patients?'[15] The chief means of discovering this are observation and discussion. The acts of a psychotic are often determined by social factors and one must therefore look beyond the smokescreen of their phantasies. And yet one must remember that their phantasies are real to them, and that we all have some kind of phantasy life.

The following example of the interaction of phantasy lives came in one particular hospital: we were puzzled because a 'refractory ward' became, as the saying has it, 'Bedlam', when one Sister was on duty, yet it was fairly quiet when she was off duty. The puzzle lay in watching her at work. She seemed intelligent, skilful, kind, efficient; she was somewhat masculine; she appeared well liked by the patients. What was happening?

It took weeks of talk and observation to discover that trouble followed when the Sister had an icy exchange, which she often had, with a particular very feminine nurse. This nurse had a strangely close relationship with a young psychotic girl. An 'attack' on the nurse was felt by the patient as an attack on herself. She had many other phantasies about the Sister and the nurse, seeing them as quarrelling parents, and, like a child, felt that she herself had brought about the quarrel. This made her feel guilty and anxious. She converted much of her anxiety into aggression and expressed it by smashing windows and chairs. Since she was seen by several of the other patients as a kind of leader, someone who would not conform to the rules, a kind of heroic figure, her destructive outbursts were swiftly copied by them. Gradually it was possible to work out in terms of phantasied identities and unconscious needs, of staff as well as patients, what was going on in this little community, this world, as it then was, on its own. In trying to understand the patient we had to become aware of the personalities of some of the staff. And when we understood, we could bring about therapeutic change.

There is a severe shortage of nurses and it will be impossible to humanize and modernize all our mental hospitals until this is remedied. It is the nurse who has the longest and most severe testing in any mental hospital. It is often with a nurse that a patient who was 'lost' establishes his first real relationship. The importance of the psychiatric nurse is expressed by the 'life line syndrome', as Stanton and Schwartz called it.[16] There were patients in the ward they studied who needed to have their beds near the 'nursing office'. If they were moved away from it, they produced 'schizophrenic fragmentation', which cleared again on their being moved back. The mobility of the symptoms was a much more significant observation than the existence of psychotic anxieties and phantasies themselves. As the physical and social aspects of a ward improved, so did the patients' behaviour. 'Episodes of explosive violence and outbursts of hyperkinetic activity, the so-called schizophrenic "acting-out", began to disappear with the elimination of ward "evils" and the substitution of social programmes.'[17] Dr D. H. Clark believes that the social upheavals of the 1939–45 war, in which psychiatrists were taken out of the 'closed worlds' of their mental hospitals and the 'cosiness' of their consulting rooms and were plunged into the turmoil of different situations, made them forcibly aware of the tremendous influence of social factors on men's thinking and feeling.[13] Out of this awareness grew group psychotherapy, community methods of treatment, and social psychiatry in general. At first, these new techniques were applied in war or immediately post-war situations, such as in rehabilitation units for ex-prisoners of war, where the basic emotional problems were demoralization and desocialization, and where neurotic rather than psychotic illness was involved. The United Kingdom has a particularly distinguished record of pioneering both in this early phase, and later, when the techniques came to be applied to communities of psychotics. Dr Maxwell Jones started working in the early phase. He later applied the treatment methods to psychopaths – abnormally aggressive, or seriously irresponsible people, but not psychotic, who are notoriously difficult to treat individually. Dr Jones commented, 'our findings appear to justify the conclusion that it is possible to change social attitudes in relatively desocialized patients with severe character disorders, provided they are treated together in a therapeutic community'.[18] He has gone on to run Dingleton Hospital on the same lines, with psychotic as well as neurotic and psychopathic patients.

It is immensely interesting to see that if psychopaths are placed in a milieu in which every anti-social act is subject to discussion and sanction by all the members of the small, special community in which they live, some of them eventually learn to behave in a more socially acceptable way. The patients are under constant observation and, therefore, control, of their peers and the community staff. The 'therapeutic community' in the form devised by Maxwell Jones has not been used in a widespread fashion in treating psychosis. The name 'therapeutic community', however, has come to stand for 'an attitude, and a method, a system of treatment and a battle cry, a charm and a password'. From it has largely emerged the social therapy of psychosis.

At the basis of social therapy is the *concept of culture*, where the term is used to mean the traditions and values shared by a particular limited community. It is for this reason that key books on mental hospitals now use the language of sociology and social anthropology. It is no mere jargon, or new names for old problems, when a study calls itself *The Culture of the State Mental Hospital*[19] or *The Psychiatric Hospital as a Small Society.*[20] Asylums have, of course, always been societies; a few enlightened ones had quite a degree of complexity and richness in particular phases of progressive administration. Hanwell Asylum, famous in history books for being the hospital where John Conolly, who died a hundred years ago, introduced the system of 'no restraint', even had its own brewery at one time and a variety of workshops. But in the immediate past the majority of hospitals by their very design and administration denied the 'social instinct' that, mad or sane, we all possess.

One of the classical descriptions of a therapeutic community is

an attempt to use a hospital not as an organization run by doctors in the interest of their own greater technical efficiency, but as a community with the immediate aim of full participation of all its members in its daily life. . . . Ideally, it has been conceived as a therapeutic setting, with a spontaneous and emotionally structured (rather than medically dictated) organization in which all staff and patients engage.[21]

This quotation is very relevant to the treatment of psychotics. Indeed, Dr Main, whom we have just quoted, went on to discuss the necessity for the community he was describing to provide for special needs such as a secluded place to mourn. That is to say, such a community should be able to contain and support individuals having depressive experiences.

The way in which social therapy is most appropriate for psychosis is that, even though the psychotic's ability to maintain interpersonal relationships can be greatly damaged, they are nevertheless important to him. Wilfred Trotter believed that the social instinct was the 'very foundation of society'. He thought the gregarious animal was 'different from the solitary one in the capacity to become conscious in a special way of the existence of other creatures. He is able to feel with the other and share his pleasures and sufferings as if they were an attenuated form of his own personal experiences.'[22] Self-evident as this may seem, it has only very recently been applied to thinking about psychotic communities. Because a very mad person is often unable to benefit from individual psychotherapy, as he cannot relate well enough, it was thought that he did not relate at all. However, the argument should be that if damaged relating to others is a large part of the illness, then relating itself must be at one of the principal foci of therapeutic treatment. And if one person – even a psychiatrist – is unable to use the tenuous relating ability of the psychotic constructively, then multiplying the number of therapeutic contacts the patient has, creating as coherent and sensitive a social matrix as possible, is a better therapeutic answer; increasing the psychotic's social isolation certainly is not.

In an appropriate environment the well-organized ego of a normal person acts with a sense of confidence in the persistence both of itself and of its environment.[23] The disorganized ego of the psychotic is beset with phantasy and with problems of realistic communication both with the outer and the inner worlds, problems based on the difficulty of distinguishing between phantasy and fact. The psychotic gains no confidence from the persistence of what seems to him a strange inner and outer world. The very persistence of these altered worlds constitute his madness. His realities are also unreal to us. Our task in helping him lies in giving him as much opportunity for 'reality-testing' – checking his subjective experiences against the really real world – as possible. What does this mean in practical terms? What characteristics of an environment can help the psychotic? Ideally the milieu must 'offer the patient a clear, organized, unambiguous social structure, problems to solve in protected situations and a variety of settings in which to solve these problems'.[23] The Cummings, whom we have just quoted, go on to describe what else the environment must offer the psychotic in order to help him in 'ego restitution'. They include the presence of a 'peer group' – other patients – and of a helpful staff to encourage and assist him to live more effectively. The treatment programme should aim at equipping him to act in clearly defined roles, aided by a variety of motivating forces and governed by different cultural values. This should ideally result in an ego structure sufficiently differentiated and varied to allow a wide range of competence. Such changes in 'ego organization' would protect the patient from experiences of 'diffusion of ego feeling', that is, the loss of ego-identity, which are accompanied by all the strange distortions of the total self and of reality that we have already examined. The Cummings speak of the patient needing to learn to act in a number of *different*, but clearly defined roles, because

non-psychotic people have several separate real identities, related
to the different roles they are called on to play, now in relation
to one person or situation, now to another. Paying 'attention',
being able to concentrate and be flexible in a changing social
situation, all require different aspects of the self to come into
operation. For the non-psychotic, each situation has its own
interest – or boredom. We respond to environment not in a
random way, but quickly to some things, actively or passively,
or not at all, to others. In other words, there is a hierarchical
aspect to the organization of our egos. The way we act towards
situations varies 'in accordance to the context in which we
originally learned about such situations – in terms of the cultural
values surrounding their acquisition'.[19]

And so the psychotic requires a richness and an unambiguous
complexity in the community that is trying to lead him back to our
more generally accepted reality. The disruption of ego feeling and
ego-boundaries is, we must remember, not peculiar to schizophrenia. In depressive psychosis an emptying of the ego is felt,
a draining away of self-esteem. As the Cummings say, 'some people
seem to be more acutely aware than others are of ego-boundaries
. . . some people when in crisis suffer from feelings of alienation,
depersonalization or loss of boundary, whereas others suffer
from feelings of deflation, emptiness and collapse'. They ask
whether it is through the sense of ego-boundary that we come to
comprehend the world, and at the same time are given a 'sharp
and immediate sense of self as separate from the world, without
which action cannot proceed effectively'.

We have returned for a moment to the language we used in
earlier chapters to try to show how it can help us to understand the
patient's social needs, in terms of his internal experience. Psychoanalytic and other models can often be used to understand particular elements of 'communicating' behaviour. This, I hope, I
have illustrated by reducing symptoms to the level of infant
experience, especially of the experiences of children and infants
under emotional stress, and by the use of other 'models'. The
former physician superintendent of an asylum was often a Vic-
torian father-figure with a vengeance. His 'children', patients
and staff, obligingly produced caricatures of dependent, disturbed
living. Psychoanalytic interpretation of behaviour is often more

helpful to those caring for psychotic patients than for the patients themselves. The latter can know by their own experiences more about 'psychiatry' than their attendants do. But it is obviously important that those having to care for the psychotic should be able to take the mystery or terror out of the symptoms they see. It is also important that those who care should gain insight into problems of their own, which might otherwise further block already disturbed communication with the patient.

We have a lot of data now on what it is like to be a patient. For example, there was an experiment in which an anthropologist was admitted to a ward as a patient under a pseudonym.[24] Such are the forces at work in these 'psychotic societies' that this pseudo patient lost his objectivity. He became a member of the patient society: he identified with it. However, Dr Caudill, the anthropologist involved, later made a series of objective studies[20] of the 'transactions' that went on in the hospital – the effects of real or imaginary events, the processes that go through the society of the hospital. To understand disturbances in the hospital, interest had to focus sometimes on a single person; sometimes on one or several small groups of people and sometimes on the whole interacting hospital, with all the distortions and exaggerations that go on with humans communicating as they do.

It can seem very threatening to the staff of a mental hospital to start taking a more democratic, humanistic approach, to demolish the old hierarchical structure, so beloved of all types of institutions. It means having your own motives openly questioned. It demands a kind of emotional maturity that was never tested while you hid behind a ready-made persona – the role of the doctor with a white coat and 'instant' authority; the role of the nurse, and all the rest. Questioning motives can lead to very new points of view. Dr Atkin, in a provocative little book,[25] writes:

Certainly I have come across arguments in favour of the generous use of leucotomy which appear to be in the nature of rationalizations ... to bleach the affects by means of a leucotomy in a case of episodic depression or melancholia on the ground of relieving mental suffering is a debatable procedure ... the patient ... would as readily agree to being killed outright (suicidal tendency) ... If there is at all a chance of restitution to normality, a prolongation of the suffering is worth-while

... another argument in favour of a generous use of leucotomy is that the violent and aggressive reactions of certain types of psychotics are thus cut out and therefore these patients become an easier nursing proposition ... that is looking at it from the nurse's point of view, not the patients'.

Dr Atkin suggests that physical treatments have sometimes been used on account of the general exasperation of relatives, nurses and doctors, because the patient 'refuses' to get well. He even suggests unconscious jealousy of the 'freedom' of the psychotic on the part of those around him, who feel strain and a temptation to let go *themselves* and combat this by 'knocking out' the patient with E.C.T. or by performing a prefrontal leucotomy. Thus social therapy even tries to re-evaluate physical treatment in motivational terms. Dr Denis Martin, in an account of the task of creating a therapeutic community, wrote:

Perhaps the most important realization brought home to us by our study of the old system and by information from our patients was that in the past we have been treating people as things or, at best, as interesting diseases ... the end begins to justify the means ... A system which tends to create tensions and disturbed behaviour was called upon to suppress and control these by the same measures that originally helped to produce them. Heavier and heavier sedation, more and more frequent periods of seclusion, repeated courses of E.C.T. had to be used in many wards to maintain some sort of control over the more difficult patients who did not readily submit to hospital life. Little attempt was made to understand the behaviour in terms of the patient's human response to the total situation of ward and hospital life.[26]

Patients themselves have written a huge and strangely neglected literature[27] which can often touchingly tell us of what happens on the other side of the barriers to understanding.

Social therapy of the psychoses can therefore be divided into two sections. The commonest one, we must emphasize again, is that in which group activity and physical treatments are prominent. The rarer form we have just been attempting to characterize, rather than to describe exhaustively. Here all treatment methods are viewed just as critically as 'roles'; indeed, they are seen as the expression of the roles therapists consciously or unconsciously adopt. This second form of the therapeutic community has been, and continues to be, practical and hopeful and to influence the less psychodynamically oriented communities. Again, it should be emphasized that both types of treatment, or both approaches to treatment, can be given to in-patients or out-patients in a mental hospital, a psychiatric day hospital, or the out-patient department of a general hospital.

The task in a therapeutic community is intellectually and emotionally challenging; psychotics are incredibly sensitive to insincerity, and evangelism, like love, is not enough; but optimism has its own creativity, particularly when it is not denying. Even if we are unable to half empty our mental hospitals by 1975, as some officials optimistically forecast, social psychiatry has made great progress. Perhaps new discoveries will be made which will empty them. Meanwhile, patients can be under treatment rather than in despair. Perhaps we will have to accept as the high price of our kind of civilization a minority needing a special sub-culture of their own. It should be a dynamic, aware community, a kind of continuous experiment, feeding back to itself all its observations about itself. Such communities promise to tell us a lot about social change. Perhaps this is the next phase. Just as insight into the individual mind has had an influence on many non-psychiatric disciplines, so we may learn about the groups we all live in by learning about these special groups, where tensions are higher and phantasies more blatant.

*

In discussing the 1959 Mental Health Act, I mentioned the question of community care, responsibility for which was placed on the local authority. This raises in turn the question of what lessons have been learned about the influence of social factors on a patient's illness, factors which either contribute to his illness, or prevent him from getting, or keeping, well. As patients go in and out of hospital, or from one form of therapeutic situation to another, the question of the home situation becomes interesting and important in a way it never was when they were cut off indefinitely from their homes and from the community. Affective disorders do not generally present such problems of chronicity as schizophrenic ones can do, and we will deal with the senile psychoses in a later section. What then is the *prognosis* for a schizophrenic, taking both social factors in his home environment and the severity of his psychosis into account? If differing hospital environments can make patients worse or better, the same may be true of home environments.

Firstly, let us deal with the illness in the individual, using 'label' terms, but remembering the dangers of thinking in terms of labels alone. Schizophrenia has been held to be at its most destructive when it appears insidiously in the young. The evidence for this view is, however, not at all conclusive; some young patients develop a long illness, others not. Older and readmitted patients tend to chronicity.[28] On the other hand, a sudden, acute onset holds much more hope for a quick recovery than an insidious one. The really explosive illness that can so terrify the family in which it erupts can, in fact, be a short one followed by complete recovery. Again, a person who seems to have been 'driven mad' by obvious events in his life situation is more likely soon to become sane again than a person to whom no such precipitating factors can easily be ascribed. A person who prior to his illness had a reasonable social and work history, a fairly secure psychosexual identity and varied interests and hobbies, often has a short illness. A family history of schizo-phrenia on the one hand worsens the outlook; on the other, a history of manic-depressive illness improves it. Such symptoms as continuing bizarre mannerisms and delusions, a severe thought disorder and 'flatness of affect' are less likely to disappear, while hyperactivity and mental confusion can clear up fairly quickly, leaving little, if any, handicap behind. The length of time a person has already been ill has proved to be a valuable way of determining the probable total length of his breakdown. In these days of change there are very many different criteria used by different hospitals and individual psychiatrists for admitting or discharging patients. However, those who have been ill for less than two years before admission to hospital make a speedier recovery than those who have been ill longer.

Apart from these individual features, which help or hinder a patient in his recovery, there is still the problem of the attitude of the general community itself towards mental illness. How much tolerance will the patient find on returning to it?

Earlier in this chapter we commented on the fact that the revolution in psychiatry has led to high discharge rates of patients from hospital. This includes cases of schizophrenia. Whereas thirty years ago nearly two-thirds of patients would still remain in hospital after two years,[29] less than ten per cent now do so.[30] Nowadays, the average patient spends weeks rather than months in hospital. He may have to return to hospital, or some equivalent sheltered place, from time to time, but he will spend most of his life outside hospital. Probably the phenothiazine drugs have been the most important single contribution to therapy. It is not widely enough understood, however, that *treatment still leaves a substantial number of patients with residual symptoms*. Furthermore, among this group of *chronic* schizophrenics, drugs must continue to be taken in order to control more severe symptoms that would reappear if the drugs were discontinued. *There is a high relapse rate among patients in this group who cease to take their drugs, even if they have been on these drugs for years*.[31]

There is evidence that some schizophrenics are unable to stand, without relapse, intense or demanding personal relationships.[32]

It is for patients such as these that hostels and other forms of accommodation can prove safer for their mental health than a return home. Surroundings which make few emotional demands seem to suit many schizophrenics best on their discharge from hospital.[33]

There is often a higher rate of relapse if they return to their parents or wives than if they go to live in lodgings or stay with more distant relatives.[34] However we interpret studies of the families of schizophrenics, 'high emotional involvement' or 'low emotional involvement' in the patient's social environment has an influence on how badly or how well he gets on on returning home. It may be that the accumulation of schizophrenics in old town centres partly reflects a defensive manoeuvre on their part, an avoidance of relationships which they feel unable to deal with. (For manic depressives, on the other hand, home is the best environment.) It is important to make clear when we are *interpreting* and when we are *describing* relationships. In neither case are we moralizing or taking sides with families or patients. We need information about the symptoms patients continue showing once they are in the community, and what social adjustments are required.[35] The criteria of admission to hospital, or length of stay there, no longer serve as measures of how ill a patient is, for, as we have said, admission and discharge policies vary too much from place to place, and this is true of readmissions also. It is sometimes easier to prevent readmission to hospital than to prevent the abnormal behaviour which hitherto has made readmission necessary. On the one hand 'institutionalism' can be extremely damaging;[36] on the other, the examination of a group of schizophrenic men during the year following their discharge from hospital showed that in 59 per cent of the patients' families relations were strained, often beyond what many of us would call tolerable.[37] It was found in this careful survey that half of the patients failed to continue to take the drugs prescribed for them, and quite inadequate preventive or supportive psychiatric help was offered until a crisis point was reached. It was shown, however, that the families involved in the survey often tried to tolerate very disturbed behaviour without complaint. The authors of the survey commented that, in the absence of effective community services (such as day hospitals, or sheltered workshops) the policy of early discharge of schizophrenic patients is based to a large degree on the willingness of relatives to attempt the role of nurse and to put up with considerable discomfort and distress. Oddly enough, the survey was of patients discharged from *London* hospitals. Surveys in other regions, such as Nottingham and Croydon, where community services are better developed, show that families can receive much more effective support by these services which can be as helpful as the actual hospitalization of the patient.[38]

In London surveys readmissions to hospital of discharged patients are strikingly high – 42 per cent of cases during the fairly recent period under review.[39] It was found that readmissions could be predicted by such factors as the severity of symptoms at discharge, unconstructive attitudes on the part of the patient, a poor work record, and an intense emotional relationship between the patient and a key member of his family. In criticizing the Ten Year Hospital Plan, we remarked that it did not sufficiently allow for regional variations. We can follow this up by contrasting London with Edinburgh, where only 18 per cent of comparable patients had to be readmitted to hospital.[40] The reasons for this substantial difference in readmission rates seem to be that patients remain somewhat longer in hospital in Edinburgh, have fewer symptoms when they are discharged, and then receive better community care.

Community care continues to be the ideal of much official thinking.[41] The population of in-patients continues to fall substantially.[42] Psycho-geriatric care looms large for the near future.[42,43] Controversy continues about whether the great general progress in psychiatry has depended on social re-organization in hospitals and health services,[44] or whether physical forms of treatment are to be given the credit.[45,46] We battle on with the polarity of an organic, pill-minded psychiatry versus a more psycho-dynamic, social psychiatry. Surely, in major mental illnesses, the two views are complementary.

There is grave doubt that the predictions of 1962[47] are to be fulfilled, and as many as half our mental hospitals will be closed by 1975.[48] Our ageing population is producing an ever growing load of geriatric problems. To a lesser extent, increased in-patient facilities are still in severe shortage for disturbed children and adolescents. Thus the problems themselves are altering.

Contemporary psychiatry has a series of linked, essentially practical techniques for treatment and support. Each patient presents an individual problem, and no matter how ill he is can be offered treatment rather than custody, with a whole range of therapeutic facilities, from in-patient therapeutic communities to day hospitals, night hospitals, hostels, specially selected lodgings and sheltered employment. Though we have these techniques to hand, they are not yet available to all who need them.

Senile Psychoses and the Family

(A) OLD AGE

Some parts of the body wear out before others. If this affects the nervous system, an organic psychosis may result. For example:

He was a charming old man of seventy-nine, white-haired and with a rather distinguished air. He would seat himself at a window and look out at the street day after day. If approached by a stranger he would be effusive, acting as though he had met an old friend. He could scarcely, in fact, distinguish strangers from near relatives, and was unable to remember the names of common objects he had used all his life, such as a brush or a comb. Sometimes he became confused, especially if he happened to wake up during the night. Then he might shuffle about the house calling plaintively for help, or at other times shout angrily to be left alone by imaginary tormentors. One night he fell awkwardly and fractured his hip.

What medical, social or psychological problems are presented here? I shall first examine some aspects of the emotional settings of old age, leaving to the following chapter a consideration of treatment of some of the organic psychoses. No one came to see our patient in hospital. None of his sons and daughters, none of his grandchildren. Letters from the hospital almoner inviting and urging them to visit were ignored. This raises the question of indifference, which we touched on in the opening chapter in considering some of the obstacles to understanding.

One of the technical difficulties in discussing psychiatric problems is to avoid turning all life into a nightmare. It is difficult for us to feel our way into a strange emotional situation and then easily let it go again. One of the major intentions in training psychiatrists is to enable them to do this, or at least to make it an operation carried out at reasonably low emotional cost. We can build bridges to aid our understanding of madness; but they are bridges from one place to another, from our own remote infancy to someone else's present. We have to identify and separate our own feelings in the here and now from those of the other person, yet still be sympathetic. We must try to avoid unconsciously projecting our feelings into him and, if we do feel excessively responsible for him, we should be aware of the nature of this 'guilt'. Not all guilt is neurotic; living in a guilt culture, guilt and anxiety often guide us to reasonable action. On the other hand, neurotic, 'overdetermined' guilt may be too strong for us to face. We may therefore deny it and act towards the object of our guilt with an indifference which is hardly human. I would like to examine this indifference to see whether we can understand it further in relation to the old and the senile.

' ... a civilization which offers the ageing a distinguished or even a reasonable social role tends to produce old people of surprisingly good mental health'.[1] This quotation is somewhat open to criticism since in many primitive societies the expectation of life is low. People do not live long enough to acquire some of the illnesses our old people do. This is true to an extent of suicide rates also. The rates are highest in the elderly but in some societies few reach old age anyway, so that the incidence of suicide appears relatively low. This said, the quotation retains much truth. It is obvious that old age is a time when a variety of physical disorders become commonplace. For most people the sixties mark the beginning of retirement and the wear and tear of life begins to be felt. This is the end of middle age and the beginning of old age. Emotional disorders are equally commonplace. The majority of elderly people are reasonably well-adjusted to life as they go into their sixth and seventh decade, but a substantial minority have problems. And it is estimated that by 1972 there will be over a million persons over eighty in England alone.

The child only reaches a 'genital' sexual identity at a final level of sexual maturity, which is fully achieved from adolescence onwards. With the decline of mature sexuality, old age can bring a regression to the phase that analysts call 'anal'. This explains the fussy old body, tending to miserliness, always worried about his bowels, hypochondriacal and over-rigid. The elderly also tend to dwell on the past and become more turned in upon themselves though some become garrulous. Their range of contacts and interests lessens and they become childlike again in their egocentricity. Memory, particularly for recent events, deteriorates, as does intelligence.

Each one of these statements could be amplified. For example, the regression to anality can explain the pathetic 'dirty old man'. Equally, each statement can be contradicted by one or another splendid example of a very ancient, lively and even creative man or woman, full of wisdom and vitality.

In a paper studying elderly people referred for admission to a general hospital,[2] Dr Lloyd and a senior almoner, Mr Halsall, ask for the creation of a comprehensive geriatric service. They note how 'lack of proper hospital facilities for the elderly often results in social crippling by disease', and say that 'many had progressed to the point of personal demoralization and were partially or completely rejected by their relatives'. They also noted how well the elderly often respond to medical treatment. This is certainly true of the psychiatric disorders of the aged in an astonishingly high proportion of cases.[3] Can we try, briefly, to account for the rejection of the elderly, the 'indifference' of relations?

Melanie Klein links the desire of the child to gain power, to triumph over the parent – that is, to reverse the child-parent relationship – to the desire for the attainment of success. She notes from her clinical experience how a child can have phantasies of a time 'when he will be strong, tall and grown-up, powerful, rich and potent and father and mother will have changed into helpless children; or, in other phantasies, will be very old, weak, poor and rejected'. A phantasy of destructivity, which seems to have been matched by an event carried out in reality, can be the cause of the most intense guilt. This is because an unconscious destructive phantasy directed towards a loved person is associated with infantile, omnipotent feelings which makes the person having them think that their phantasy has *caused* the catastrophe in the real world.

In our society there is probably a tendency to over-control children. Growing up, some of them develop too strongly the normal role-reversing phantasies. At worst such exaggerated triumphant unconscious phantasies survive into adult life. They can be so powerful that when a parent does become 'old and weak and poor' the guilt in the child-who-is-now-an-adult is too great: his 'phantasy has become a fact'. Guilt of this intensity is denied, and this leads to the psychopathology of children who reject their parents. Extreme guilt can not only produce depressive illness, but can also destroy relations between generations.

At lower levels of intensity such mechanisms may merely heighten the essentially ambivalent relation between parent and child. In these cases the son or daughter is left feeling excessively guilty and anxious, with an unhappiness that helps no one. (Illness in the elderly may also alert mourning reactions in their children. Mourning, as we have shown, can also have its complications.)

There is, then, an order of events in which children relate to parents, play at times at reversing roles and eventually grow up. They often achieve adult sexuality at the time when their mothers, at any rate, are going through the change of life, losing the creative significance of sexuality. Unless parents have sublimated their own sexuality, have displaced it to some appreciable degree on to other things, they may strongly resent their children achieving an adult sexual role. Envy of the young often lies behind the criticisms of them. Destructive envy like this can poison the relationship between parents and their children. Then, in his turn, the child becomes a parent and in the later childhood of his children his own parents often begin to be dependent. *The original child may have a healthy 'parental' relationship with his own parents*, or he may be indifferent; alternatively he may be as rejecting as a phantasy-ridden infant.

Nowhere in the discussion of the psychoses can we leave out social factors. Even in the case of psychoses which clearly have a major organic cause, this remains true. The suicide rate rises sharply from the fifties onwards and social isolation seems to be an important contributory factor. That men have higher suicide rates than women is probably partly to be explained by the fact that women are more skilful at maintaining social relations, even in old age. Women are perhaps also helped by their superior verbal ability (one of the best attested psychological sex differences); they are better able thus to communicate their problems to another human.

(B) DELIRIUM

In this chapter we will be mainly concerned with two organic psychoses that affect the elderly: the acute and the chronic confusional states. No illness goes on without a social setting, of course. The setting here may be the worst back ward of an old-style asylum, or a loyal, desperately tried and puzzled family.

An *acute confusional state* can develop swiftly in an elderly person who was previously in good mental health. The cause is usually a physical disturbance of brain functioning, which is, at least potentially, reversible. The great danger is death from exhaustion before treatment can prove effective. The death-rate is as high as 40 per cent. even with modern forms of management. Thus, such an illness is a medical emergency. The physical illness behind this psychosis usually originates in some other part of the body than the nervous system although it affects the brain. A well-organized medical team can reduce the death rate strikingly; one study showed that in two units where originally 12 per cent of patients died within two weeks and 70 per cent had to be sent on to mental hospitals, skilled treatment led to 80 per cent of patients being returned safely home within seventeen days.[1]

We characterized this illness briefly in the chapter on labels as one of the states of delirium. A person's sense of time and place becomes quite disorientated. He does not know what day it is, or where he is. His level of consciousness varies from moment to moment. When apparently reasonably conscious, he is suggestible, and his memory plays tricks with him. He may even have false recollections – *paramnesia*. He seems unable either to remember things, or to record what is happening. He has severe bouts of acute fear and trembling insecurity. He may have delusional ideas of reference. He is very restless, yet aimless, unable to complete actions or thoughts; his perception is altered and at times he hallucinates. The illness is at its worst at night.

These acute confusional states have been likened to sensory deprivation experiments. The senses – seeing, hearing and so on – often become poor in old people. A reduction of the blood supply to the brain through a weakening heart, mineral imbalances, deficiencies of one sort or another, lowered oxygen levels in the brain, or structural damage to it (small strokes, for example) can produce striking sensory deprivation. The accumulation of metabolites through poor kidney function, toxaemia from infections ('toxi-confusional states'), or simply fatigue, can all complete the 'sensory isolation' of some old person. Indeed they can almost 'lose their senses'. In doing so their world becomes terrifying and almost unrecognizable. They hear voices and see dreadful visions as they hallucinate and as perception fails. Through the savage jungle of invented, unique experiences, the past and the misunderstood present waver and crash together.

Treatment aims, therefore, at dealing with the physical cause swiftly, as far as possible, and feeding back from our real world repeated, simple, unequivocal signals.

Psychological, as well as physical, factors can play a part. In the study we quoted[1] it was recorded that patients recovering from a delirious episode, which might often be a brief one, sometimes relapsed because their bed was moved, making them face an unfamiliar scene, or because a new, unfamiliar night nurse came on duty. Anything causing a feeling of unfamiliarity or isolation was harmful. It was found helpful if the nurses repeatedly explained who they were, explained the surroundings, and identified movements or noises which seemed to disturb a patient. Such simple reassurances could bring relief from fear and he might drop off to sleep. Since a new, unfamiliar environment is so bad for the patient, it follows that the place to treat acute confusional states is, as far as possible, the patient's own home.

Community care of the aged is obviously relevant, and preventive measures, such as improved housing, occupation, and activities of one sort or another, can all help to save the aged from isolation and self-neglect. Regular medical check-ups are important. I would like to see special cheap telephone rates for retired people to help reduce their social isolation. A doctor should be able to prescribe a telephone for a patient, especially a crippled one.

From the practical point of view, then, this kind of delirium is best treated at home. It must inevitably cause some upset in the family, because it is a serious physical illness. However, it is often treatable and a full range of modern drugs, from antibiotics to tranquillizers, is available. Since delirium is so often nocturnal it can bring a family to its knees with exhaustion, if through 'pride', shame or ignorance it fails to seek help and tries to cope without medical help.

In nursing a delirious patient, as few environmental changes as possible should be made. Explanations of simple things that seem to disturb the patient may have to be made many times over. A discussion of the well-remembered past can reassure. At night, especially, reassurance is needed. Patients should have their own familiar things about them. As shadows seem to act in a peculiarly threatening way, their bedrooms should be lit at night. If the patient has had to be sent into hospital, short visits by the family will be helpful.

*

Over the last fifty years the number of people in the United Kingdom over sixty years of age has trebled. This is almost entirely due to a reduction in infant mortality. The average expectation of life has hardly increased at all for those of fifty years of age. 'Psychiatric illness is probably the largest single cause of chronic infirmity in senescence.'[2] Of these psychiatric illnesses we are now only going to consider *chronic confusional states*, but these are an increasing social problem because of the numbers of elderly people in the country. These states take two main forms: *senile dementia*, which is caused by a premature death of nerve cells in the brain, and *arteriosclerotic dementia*, where there is a more patchy damage to the brain, caused by the degeneration of blood vessels supplying it. Dementia can give rise to medico-legal problems of testamentary capacity: a demented person may make out a will and sign it. This can lead to all sorts of wrangles concerning the state of mind he was in when he did so, whether the will is valid, and so on.

Senile dementia is more than a mere caricature of ageing. It is a progressive, massive deterioration of the personality. There is a marked disturbance of memory. At first this is usually only of recent events and particularly names, while the memory for remote times remains intact. Patients may recount in overwhelming detail things that happened to them in their childhood, while they are perhaps quite incapable of remembering the name of the street they live in. As understanding and judgement are lost, they become more childish and egocentric. With the decrease in intellectual ability comes a narrowing of interests and eventually poverty of thought and emotional regression. They may become apathetic, or, alternatively, irritable, peevish and restless.

The brain continues to lose its original computor-like ability. It becomes less and less able to 'code, store and transmit information'. Adaptability goes, and as the illness increases in intensity, contact with reality is lost. The individual lives more and more in a private world that begins to be invaded by hallucinations and delusions. There may be episodes of acute confusion, especially at night, and wandering and getting lost. Disorientation emerges and memory of even remote events disintegrates.

At different stages different problems arise. The memory disturbance can lead a patient to forget where he left something he values. If much persecutory anxiety has been released in his emotional regression, he may well accuse someone of stealing from him. Personal conduct deteriorates, sometimes exaggerating a previous minor abnormality of the personality, which leads, for example, to stealing or sexual troubles. A sexual misdemeanour may be the first symptom to bring attention to the illness. Personal cleanliness becomes increasingly neglected. Incontinence can occur early in the illness, and, as a leading text on the mental diseases of the aged acknowledges, 'many patients have to be extricated from conditions of unbelievable filth when removed to hospital'.[3] Hypochondriasis can be very marked and it may be difficult to reassure the patient that his bowels are not blocked up, or that some other part of his body is not the site of some physical catastrophe.

Senile dementia is commoner in women than in men, and usually develops in the seventies. It means that deterioration of the brain in old age has gone on faster than the dilapidation of the rest of the body. Yet, as with all the other psychoses, we cannot consider the individual as separate from the society he lives in. The physical basis of this psychosis is itself not clear cut. There can be extensive, detectable brain pathology with few mental symptoms, or slight physical pathology with severe mental symptoms. It has been suggested that the reason for these variations is the 'capacity of the personality to compensate for the brain damage'.[4] Since the personality depends on contact with others, social factors are important even in what might be thought of as one of the most organic psychoses. Among the socio-economic factors are found: 'Poverty, loneliness, faulty nutrition, poor living conditions and family disharmony, any or all of which may be of equal importance, if not greater importance' than organic factors.[5]

In confusional states the 'latest developed and the least organized' of mental qualities are the ones first lost. Personal identity,

as we have used the term, crashes into reverse and into fragments. The individual continues to try to make what sense he
can of his experiences. Once, as we all do, he might have 'ration-
alized', deceiving himself by giving himself socially acceptable
reasons for his behaviour, which had perhaps unworthy, but certainly unconscious motivation. Now he may *confabulate:* foolish-
ly or plausibly filling in the great gaps in his recent memory, in-
venting experiences. He will monotonously repeat stories from
the remote past. On the one hand he asks for help in his depen-
dency; but at the same time he tries, pathetically, to assert his
authority. As all his earlier identities re-emerge, behaviour we
could take for granted in an infant can appal us in an old man or
woman. On losing its intellect a personality, adult because its
instincts have been intellectualized, releases again its primitive
forms of anxiety. Thus some demented patients become paranoid, suspicious and apprehensive. Others are so depressed that
they can be suicidal. Mania can develop so that a physically fragile person is full of absurd confidence and cheerfulness.

For all this, and in spite of the high death-rate, many senile
dements are treatable. Early, mild cases can be treated at home;
the noisy, violent or restless – and of course those living alone –
must probably go to hospital. Skilled nursing on the lines we
suggested helpful for acute confusional states is helpful here.
With planned rehabilitation, an appreciable number of old people
improve markedly. Any somatic illness must be discovered and
dealt with. Confining elderly people to bed is a dangerous practice, bad for old joints and hearts. The general health of the old
almost always demands their being up and about for some time of
the day. Stairs and polished floors are dangerous. Gentle exercise and some light occupation can tranquillize. The help of a
social worker can mobilize personal family resources. Many of
the nursing problems are like those of caring for a toddler, and
may include toilet training. Tranquillizers are effective and can
diminish agitation without 'doping'. All these measures can lead
to a large number of patients who have had 'degraded' habits
for months being clean and dry.

The other chronic confusion – arteriosclerotic dementia –
affects more men than women and a younger age group. Damage
to the brain depends on excessively high blood pressure or hard-

ening of the arteries of the brain; the two combine eventually.

The confusional illness may begin with a fit. Early symptoms often include dizziness and tiring easily. Vague headaches and difficulty in getting to sleep are common. Memory for recent events, and particularly for names, becomes impaired. In conversation such patients show a marked difficulty in switching from one subject to another. They may have morbid preoccupations with imaginary bodily ailments, and they have the 'labile affect' of an organic psychosis. Apart from this, they are frequently irritable and depressed.

Even at this stage of the illness the personality is still very well preserved. The symptoms themselves vary very much from one time to another, but although he is aware of them and distressed by them, the person goes on. From time to time a clouding of consciousness appears lasting a few days then clearing again. Eventually the dementia may be profound, with complete disorientation, and even hallucinations and delusions. *Aphasia* may be shown. When an individual does not understand spoken or written words he suffers, we say, from *receptive aphasia*. When he cannot speak or write he has *expressive aphasia*.

The fluctuating course of sclerotic dementia contrasts with senile dementia. The prognosis, in the short term at any rate, and particularly for women, is much better. Treatment must be given for excessive blood pressure, where this exists.

Emotional factors can also be dealt with. The advent of the anti-depressive drugs is important here.[6] E.C.T. temporarily impairs the memory for recent events and in the past was rarely used as treatment for a depressed patient already having trouble with his memory.[7] Tranquillizers can deal with agitation. As far as possible the 'cerebral arteriopath' should continue his ordinary life. Regular medical care which includes a 'relationship' with the doctor and his team is important. The self-driving, over-conscientious person must learn to lower his sights, yet not give up.

Many people are worried by hearing that they have 'blood pressure'. An indication of this is that the lay expression 'I've got blood pressure' is widely used to name an 'illness'. It takes an expert physician to judge the significance of a *raised* blood pressure. It can often be symptomless – until the patient is told he has it.

*

All the diseases of old age are now being given more attention. Standards of care vary very much from one part of the country to another, however. The problem is not simply medical, but medico-social. The National Assistance Act (1948) made it the responsibility of local authorities to provide 'accommodation for persons who by reason of age, infirmity or other circumstances are in need of care and attention not otherwise available to them'. This has yet to happen nation-wide. Home helps, friends, voluntary organizations, social workers, all these are part of 'social medicine'. The problems of ageing often begin many years before retirement is reached. Research into the prevention of catastrophic personality deterioration among the aged goes on.

In my clinical experience I have met very depressed women who had nursed their own demented mothers or fathers, with little or no medical help, until the latter died. The distortion of family life by this burden was almost unbearable, and the subsequent guilt when the problem ended severe. Pent up frustration and aggression can have a very devastating effect on the survivor.

Again, psychogeriatric facilities and welfare services are vitally important. Small quantities of drugs, skilfully employed, may help a whole family in helping its newly dependent member. Short stays in hospital for the purposes of rehabilitation can also give a family a well-deserved break. The doctor must be able to judge how much a family can take and be prepared to urge hospitalization when the problem becomes too great.

*

A person must go on being treated as human if he is to remain human. The range of drugs that give support without dehumanizing, that allay anxiety without reducing a person to a sleepy vegetable, is increasing. Drugs designed to raise the mood or reduce feelings of persecution continue to become safer and more predictable in their effect. All these, with the aid of modern *physical* treatment, provide half the answer to the problems of delirium. The other half lies in the response of the community.

Because the second childhood has less promise than the first we should not care less about those who are passing through it. We ourselves are part of the treatment of old age.

Part Four

Conclusions

In order to understand madness, we have to understand human nature, for madness is relative to this and arises from it. This is why I have built this book around a model of human development. We all have an idea of human nature, generalizing from ourselves and from our own particular life experiences. This is usually a commonsense view. It tends to be too rational and too respectable a view both as regards other people and ourselves. It may seem that psychiatrists are tiresomely complicating things when they offer their explanatory systems. My own psycho-dynamic structure may seem complicated. Yet what they try to explain is not simple; no one simply goes mad, and when they are mad simple explanations of their behaviour are useless. Simple explanations are therapeutically at best inert, and at worst destructive.

All humans belong to the same biological race: any differences are too unimportant *scientifically* to enable anyone to define separate biological races.[1] On the other hand, ethnology – the study of social relations, customs and cultures in different human groups – reveals differences even in madness, between not only the types of disturbances different populations themselves think of as odd, but also in the frequency of these disturbances. The latter is often unreliably reported, because of varying cultural biases. Nevertheless, even allowing for these distortions, real differences in frequency remain. This shows the importance of cultural factors in the development of madness. We have to be very careful in generalizing about human nature. In discussing the commoner forms of madness, we have been concerned with our own society, which is itself a multiple society. We must acknowledge this, even though we realize that madness has also an absolute aspect, related to a universal norm. Part of our fear of madness is, I think, linked to our fears of violence and death, and our internal problems of depressive and persecutory anxiety. With world wars and concentration camps such recent history, and violence going on in the present, why should we believe that irrational man can improve?[2] Yet we must turn to detailed *evidence* for answers about our 'nature', a nature which can be so different in different cultures. Suicide, for example, is a problem of complex, affluent countries, rather than simpler primitive ones; and there is a tendency for the suicide rate to vary inversely with the homicide rate.[3] Thus, our low homicide rates in the United Kingdom are 'bought', in a sense, at the expense of high suicide rates: in our society aggression is turned most often on the self.*[4]

Wild generalizations have been made about Nazi Germany and the intrinsic brutality of human nature;[5] but Germany has its own culture, different from ours. There is evidence that Adolf Hitler and his movement were bewitched by the ideas of Nietzsche, Machiavelli and de Sade:[6] these ideas have never really seemed anything but sick to us. Yet we would be foolish to forget the sadism of the remoter historical past, or the existence of other more cruel cultures in the present. We all belong to the same species; we all are potentially alike. There is, therefore, something sensibly selfish in supporting the constructive agencies in our community. For all the self-criticism we now go in for, fumbling our way into a second industrial revolution, and adjusting to being a small country without an Empire, this is quite a safe country to live in compared with various others, in that we are safe from attack from others in the street or in the home. Thus North American problems, for example, bear no direct relevance to those found in Britain. Despite what we said of homicide and suicide rates being generally inversely related to one another, in the U.S.A. there are sixty times as many murders per year as in the U.K., even though their population is only four times larger; yet they have the same suicide rates as ourselves. It is more important, therefore, to accumulate precise facts about particular populations and to compare these, than to generalize from one

---

*Konrad Lorenz in his brilliant, important and pessimistic book *Aggression* (Methuen, 1966) seems to neglect this factor.

group for all mankind. And the groups must be small enough for us to know what we are doing.[7] The American figures, for example, become more understandable when we examine the ethnic troubles that they have:[3] gross inequalities are dangerous.

Everyone thinks himself an expert on human nature. There is, it is true, the *art* of medicine, which in psychiatry can and must be shared by non-medical people – psychiatric social workers, lay psychotherapists, art-therapists and sensitive, intuitive, interested lay individuals. But we have progressed beyond uninformed 'common sense'. Medicine is a science, as well as an art. Psychiatry has a scientific, experimental aspect as intellectually challenging as any other science and far more broadly based.[8] Facts about our culture are as necessary as feelings. Psychiatry has not only grown as a body of knowledge, but is mature enough to engage now in the criticism of its own various schools, as we saw in discussing social psychiatry. Its differences provide growing points, as well as correctives to the more exaggerated schools.

The modern emphasis is on behaviour and social interaction. Our goal is also to understand the patient's experiences. A major nervous breakdown, a psychosis, follows a complex social rejection and misunderstanding; admission to mental hospital follows social breakdown and social isolation, rather than just an increase in severity of symptoms, though obviously one can lead to another. We can see psychosis as an emotional immaturity, relative to the norms of a particular culture; the mad, the crazy, the lunatic are also, however, people who can express and experience anxiety in grossly more primitive ways than we do. Psychotic anxieties, infantile in form, are also related to the emotional needs of children. Different kinds of anxieties respond to different drugs and thus persecutory and depressive anxieties, for example, are not merely metaphysical terms and we are able to link body and mind, words and madness, drugs and symptoms.

Considering psychotic deviation from a biological, intra-psychic, interpersonal and cultural point of view, measures such as leucotomy seem to me desperate. Again, ethics will be involved if ever we close the distance between a 'gene' and its effects: control of the genetics of behaviour will involve more than psychiatric considerations.

Electroplexy has been called helping 'the patient to commit
suicide without dying' and to hate 'without murder';[9] certainly
it is an empirical form of treatment. Both the writer quoted and
others acknowledge that the symptoms of an endogenous depressive illness are improved by E.C.T. Yet the patient may not
develop a sense of *complete* recovery until weeks or months
later.[10] It does not seem unreasonable to class E.C.T. as a dramatic form of psychotherapy. The patient finds he survives a ritual-
ized suicide and murder. His omnipotent phantasies of his own
destructivity are tested and are shown to be real impulses, yet
also to be only phantasies, because he survives. Some patients
seem only to see the treatment as punishment; this is where the
'treatment' is not offered within a human relationship, and
where a psychiatrist has not, perhaps, 're-examined his role' in
the way we discussed in the section on social psychiatry.

Given the size of the problem of mental illness, many authorities think that the *prevention* of mental ill-health should take
priority. They suggest that psychiatrists, so few in number, would
be best deployed mainly in community programmes designed for
this, rather than trying directly to treat individuals, or even
groups of the mentally sick.[11] In my opinion the economics of
mental illness, in terms of work time lost, even apart from the
more vital question of the suffering involved where the treatment
of a patient is neglected, makes programmes of both treatment
and prevention an investment the community cannot afford to dis-
regard. Country-wide services are vitally necessary for economic
as well as humane reasons. We know what to do about madness,
if only we have the facilities. We have outlined these facilities,
but we have said little about training. The general practitioner
can be, and often is, a key figure in helping a disturbed family.
He may know it better than any social agency could. Yet with
dreary regularity the journals comment on 'the lack of preparation for this role during undergraduate medical training ... post-
graduate instruction can only partially remedy it.'[12] The attempt
to heal the huge split between the facilities provided for the
physically ill and the mentally ill is, however, under way.

Part of the work lies in the future in that there is still a split in
medicine itself. The public, I often feel, is ahead of the doctors in
this respect. Despite all this, psychiatry has shown that it can help

the psychotic in a practical way, and that it cares about the quality of people's lives. Facts and figures support these views.

The mad are only our own childhood distant from us. We learn to become parents, able to transmit our civilization to our children. Part of this civilization includes accepting those who cannot always see the changing world as we do.

References

Introduction: *Obstacles to Understanding*

1.(a) ARGYLE, M., *Psychology and Social Problems*, Methuen, 1964, pp. 38–9.

   (b) SPROTT, W. J. H., *Human Groups*, Penguin Books, 1958.

2. MILLS, E., *Living with Mental Illness. A Study in East London*, Routledge, 1962.

3. PAUL, B. D., *Health, Culture and Community*, Russell Sage, New York, 1955.

4. CUMMING, J. and E., *Closed Ranks*, Harvard University Press, 1957.

5. *Royal Commission on Medical Education 1965–8: Report*, Cmnd 3369, H.M.S.O., 1968.

6. (a) Department of Health and Social Security, *Future Structure of the National Health Service*, H.M.S.O., 1970.

   (b) Consultative Document on the above, 1971.

7. *Seebohm Report*, H.M.S.O., 1968.

8. *British Journal of Psychiatry*, vol. 119, no. 548, xxi.

9. Department of Health and Social Security, *Better Services for the Mentally Handicapped*, H.M.S.O., 1971.

10. *Public Expenditure to 1975–76*, Cmnd 4829, H.M.S.O., 1971.

11. 'Psychiatric Needs', *British Medical Journal*, 1968, vol. 2, no. 320.

12. *Psychiatric Nursing: Today and Tomorrow*, Report of the Joint Sub-Committee on the Standing Nursing Advisory Committees, Ministry of Health and Central Health Services Council, H.M.S.O., 1968.

Chapter 1 – *Normal, Neurotic, Psychotic*

1. JONES, E., *Life and Work of Sigmund Freud*, Penguin Books, 1964.

2. ACKERKNECHT, E. H., *A Short History of Psychiatry*, Hafner, New York and London, 1959.

3. MAYER-GROSS, SLATER and ROTH, *Clinical Psychiatry*, 2nd edn, Cassell, 1960, p. 8.

4. HENDERSON, D. and GILLESPIE, R. D., *Textbook of Psychiatry*, 9th edn by Henderson and Batchelor, Oxford University Press, 1962.

5. (a) KETY, S. S., *Science*, 1959, 129, 1528, 1590.
   (b) *Aspects of Psychiatric Research*, ed. D. Richter *et al.*, Oxford University Press, 1962, chapter 16.

6. BENEDETTI, G., KIND, H. and JOHANSSEN, A. S., *Fortschritte der Neurologie, Psychiatrie und ihrer Grenzgebiete*, 1962, 30, 341, 445.

7. FREUD, A., *The Ego and the Mechanisms of Defence*, Hogarth Press, 1948, p. 467.

8. FREUD, S., *An Outline of Psychoanalysis*, Hogarth Press, 1959.

9. FREEMAN, T., CAMERON, J. L. and MCGHIE, *Chronic Schizophrenia*, Tavistock, 1958.

10. FITZGERALD, F. SCOTT, *The Last Tycoon*, Penguin Books, 1960, p. 89.

11. STENGEL, E., *Bulletin of the World Health Organization*, 1959, 21, 601.

Chapter 2 – Labels

1. KRAEPELIN, E., *Psychiatry*, 8th edn, Leipzig, 1913.

2. WOOLF, L., *Beginning Again*, Hogarth Press, 1964, pp. 76, 164.

3. ANTHONY, J. and SCOTT, P., 'Manic Depressive Psychosis in Childhood', *Journal of Child Psychology and Psychiatry*, 1, 53–7, January, 1960.

4. (a) LEWIS, A. J., *Journal of Mental Science*, 1934, 80, 277.
   (b) GARMANY, G., *British Medical Journal*, 1958, 2, 341.

5. BLEULER, E., *Dementia Praecox or the Group of Schizophrenias*, International Universities Press, New York, 1911.

6. FISH, F. J., *Schizophrenia*, John Wright & Sons, 1962.

7. (a) GOLDSTEIN, K., 'Methodological Approach to the Study of Schizophrenic Thought Disorder', *Language and Thought in Schizophrenia*, ed. J. S. Kasanin, University of California Press, 1944.
   (b) GOLDSTEIN, K. and SCHEERER, M., 'Abstract and Concrete Behaviour', *Psychological Monogram 53*, no. 239, 1941.

8. MAYER-GROSS, SLATER and ROTH, *Clinical Psychiatry*, 2nd edn, Cassell, 1960.

9. DOMINIAN, J., *Psychiatry and the Christian*, Burns & Oates, 1962.

10. HENDERSON, D. and GILLESPIE, R. D., *Textbook of Psychiatry*, 9th edn by Henderson and Batchelor, Oxford University Press, 1962, p. 103.

11. FREUD, S., *An Outline of Psychoanalysis*, Tavistock, 1958.

12. PASAMANICK, B., DINITY, S. and SEFTON, M., 'Psychiatric Orientation and its Relation to Diagnosis in a Mental Hospital', *American Journal of Psychiatry*, 1959, 116, 127.

13. CREAK, E. M., *et al.*, 'Schizophrenic Syndrome in Children', *British Medical Journal*, 1961, 2, 889–90.

14. Mental Deficiency Section Working Party on Childhood Psychosis, Royal Medico-Psychological Association, 1961–2.

15. (*a*) KANNER, L., *Child Psychiatry*, 2nd edn, C. C. Thomas, U.S.A., 1953.

(*b*) WING, L., *Autistic Children*, National Association for Mental Health, 1965.

16. PUGH, J. F., JERATH, B. K. *et al.*, *New England Journal of Medicine*, 1963, 268, 1224.

17. 'Chemical Intoxications and Addictions', chapter 18, p. 336, in 8 above.

Chapter 3 – *Cultural Influences*

1. KARDINER, A., *The Psychological Frontiers of Society*, Columbia University Press, 1945.

2. BENEDICT, R., *Patterns of Culture*, Routledge, 1935.

3. OPLER, M. R., *Culture, Psychiatry and Human Values*, Springfield, 1956.

4. LEWIS, N. D. C. and CHEEK, F. E., 'Psychoanalysis and Social Science', *Modern Concepts of Psychoanalysis*, ed. L. Salzman, Peter Owen, 1962. Useful bibliography.

5. MEAD, M., *Male and Female*, Penguin Books, 1962.

6. DE BEAUVOIR, S., *The Second Sex*, Jonathan Cape, 1956.

7. ERIKSON, E., *Childhood and Society*, 2nd edn, Norton, New York, 1963. Penguin Books, 1965.

8. YOUNG, KIMBALL, *Handbook of Social Psychology*, Routledge, 1957.

9. LIN, TSUNG-YI and STANLEY, C. C., 'The Scope of Epidemiology in Psychiatry', *World Health Organization, Health Paper 16*, 1962.

10. HALMOS, P., *Towards a Measure of Man*, Routledge, 1957.

11. SHERMAN, M. and I. C. in BENTLEY, M. and COWDRAY, E. V., *The Problem of Mental Disorder*, 1934.

12. LUCAS, J., SAINSBURY, P. and COLLINS, J., *Journal of Mental Science*, vol. 108, no. 457.

13. HARE, E. H., 'Masturbatory Insanity: The History of An Idea', *Journal of Mental Science*, vol. 108, no. 452.

14. KLAF, F. S. and HAMILTON, J. G., 'Schizophrenia – A Hundred

Years Ago and Today', *Journal of Mental Science*, vol. 107, no. 450.

15. MILLS, E., *Living with Mental Illness*, Routledge, 1962.

16. BARNETT, S. A., 'Lessons from Animal Behaviour for the Clinician', *Little Club Clinics in Developmental Medicine*, no. 7, Heinemann, 1962.

17. STENSTEDT, A., 'A Study in Manic-Depressive Psychoses. Clinical, Social and Genetic Investigations', *Acta Psychiatrica Supplementa*, 79, 1952.

18. HARE, E. H., 'The Distribution of Mental Illness in the Community', chapter 3 in *Aspects of Psychiatric Research*, ed. D. Richter, Oxford University Press, 1962.

19. (a) CLARK, R. E., 'Psychosis, Income and Occupational Prestige', *American Journal of Sociology*, 1949, 54, 433–40.
    (b) HARE, E. H., 'Mental Illness and Social Conditions in Bristol', *Journal of Mental Science*, 1956, 102, 349–57.
    (c) LIN, T., 'A study of the Incidence of Mental Disorder in Chinese and other Cultures', *Psychiatry*, 1953, 16, 313–36.

20. (a) HOLLINGSHEAD, A. B. and REDLICH, F. C., *Social Class and Mental Illness*, Wiley, New York, 1958.
    (b) KAHN, R. L., POLLACK, M. and FINK, M., 'Social-psychologic aspects of psychiatric treatment in a voluntary mental hospital; duration of hospitalization, discharge ratings and diagnosis', *Archives of General Psychiatry*, American Medical Association, 1959, 1, 565.

21. TERMAN, L. M. and ODEN, M. H., *The gifted group at mid-life; thirty-five years follow-up of the superior child*, Stanford University Press, 1959.

22. ØDEGAARD, Ø., 'A statistical investigation of the incidence of mental disorder in Norway', *Psychiatric Quarterly*, 1946, 20, 381–99.

23. WING, J. K., *et al.*, 'Morbidity in the Community of Schizophrenic Patients Discharged from London Mental Hospitals in 1959', *British Journal of Psychiatry*, 1964, 110, 10–21.

24. WILHELM, R. and JUNG, C. G., *The Secret of the Golden Flower*, Kegan Paul, 1931.

25. REIK, T., 'Ritual', *Four Psychoanalytic Studies*, Evergreen Books, 1962.

26. (a) RYCROFT, C., ed., *Psychoanalysis Observed*, Constable, 1966.
    (b) STORR, A., 'The Concept of Cure', *Psychoanalysis Observed*, p. 51.

27. RUSSELL, B., *A History of Western Philosophy*, Allen & Unwin, 1963.

28. DUNHAM, B., *Man Against Myth*, Muller, 1948.

Chapter 4a – *The Earliest Social Situation*

1. KLEIN, M., *Envy and Gratitude*, Tavistock, 1957.
2. BOWLBY, J., 'The Nature of the Child's Tie to his Mother', *International Journal of Psychoanalysis*, 1958, 34, part 5. Note excellent references therein.
3. (a) BOWLBY, J., 'Maternal Care and Mental Health', *World Health Organization, Monograph Series*, Geneva, 1951.
   (b) 'Deprivation of Maternal Care', *World Health Organization, Public Health Paper 14*, 1962.
   (c) BROWN, EPPS and MCGLASHEN, *Proceedings of Third World Congress of Psychiatry*, 1963.
   (d) HILYARD and NEWMAN, 'Early Parental Deprivation as a Functional Factor in the Etiology of Schizophrenia and Alcoholism,' *American Journal of Orthopsychiatry*, vol. 33, no. 3, April 1963.
   There are many other comparable studies besides (c) and (d).
4. SUTTIE, I. D., *The Origins of Love and Hate*, Kegan Paul, 1935. Penguin Books, 1963.
5. KLEIN, M., *et al.*, *Developments in Psychoanalysis*, Hogarth Press, 1952.
6. KLEIN, M., *Contributions to Psychoanalysis*, Hogarth Press, 1950.
7. (a) STORR, A., *The Integrity of the Personality*, Penguin Books, 1963.
   (b) GLOVER, E. and BALE, J., *Psychoanalysis*, Medical Publications Ltd, 1939.
8. FREUD, S., *An Outline of Psychoanalysis*, Hogarth Press, 1938.
9. DEUTSCH, F., *Body, Mind and the Sensory Gateways*, Basic Books, 1962.
10. FREUD, S., *Mourning and Melancholia*, Standard Edition of Complete Psychological Works, vol. 14, Hogarth Press, 1957.
11. COSMAN, M., and KELLER, H., *Stravinsky at Rehearsal*, Dobson, 1962.

Chapter 4b – *The Origins of Feelings of Persecution*

1. KRETSCHMER, E., *Physique and Character*, 2nd edn revised by Miller, Routledge, 1936.
2. FREUD, S., *Beyond the Pleasure Principle*, Hogarth Press, 1950.
3. KLEIN, M., *Envy and Gratitude*, Tavistock, 1957.
4. KLEIN, M., *et al.*, *Developments in Psychoanalysis*, Hogarth Press, 1952.
5. FAIRBAIRN, W. and RONALD, D., *Psychoanalytic Studies of the Personality*, Tavistock, 1952.

6. KLEIN, M., *et al.*, *New Directions in Psychoanalysis*, Tavistock, 1955, p. 311.

7. SEGAL, H., *Introduction to the Work of Melanie Klein*, Heinemann, 1964, p. 44.

8. HUMPHREY, G., *Thinking*, Methuen, 1951.

9. BERNSTEIN, B., 'Aspects of Language and Learning in the Genesis of the Social Process', *Journal of Child Psychology and Psychiatry*, 1, 313–24, June 1966.

10. BION, W., 'Attacks on Linking', *International Journal of Psychoanalysis*, 1959, 40.

11. SCHAFFER, L., LYMAN, C. *et al.* 'On the Nature and Sources of the Psychiatrist's Experience with the Family of the Schizophrenic', *Psychiatry*, 1962, 25, 32–45.

12. ACKERMAN, N. W., *The Psychodynamics of Family Life*, Basic Books, 1958, p. 45.

Chapter 4c – *Feelings of Loss: Mourning and Depression*

1. AMBROSE, S., 'The Age of Onset of Ambivalence in Early Infancy: Indications from the Study of Laughing', *Journal of Child Psychology and Psychiatry*, 1963, 4, 167–81.

2. KLEIN, M., 'Mourning and its Relation to Manic-Depressive States', *Contributions to Psychoanalysis 1921–1945*, Hogarth Press, 1950.

3. LORENZ, K., quoted by R. A. Hinde in 'Sensitive Periods and Development of Behaviour', p. 25, *Little Club Clinics in Developmental Medicine*, no. 7, ed. S. A. Barnett, Heinemann, 1962. Note excellent references therein.

4. FOSS, B. M., ed., *New Horizons in Psychology*, Penguin Books, 1966, p. 50.

5. (*a*) SARTRE, J.-P., *Being and Nothingness*, Methuen, 1957.
   (*b*) TUSTIN, F., 'A Significant Element in the Development of Autism: A Psychoanalytic Approach', *Journal of Child Psychology and Psychiatry*, 1966, 7, 53–67.

6. FREUD, A., *The Ego and the Mechanisms of Defence*, Hogarth Press, 1961.

7. FREUD, S., *Mourning and Melancholia*, Standard Edition of Complete Psychological Works, vol. 14, Hogarth Press, 1957.

8. ABRAHAM, K., 'A Short Study of the Development of the Libido, viewed in the Light of Mental Disorder,' *Selected Papers on Psychoanalysis*, Hogarth Press, 1950.

9. BOWLBY, J., 'Childhood Bereavement and Psychiatric Illness', *Aspects of Psychiatric Research*, ed. D. Richter *et al.*, Oxford University Press, 1962

10. PARKES, C. M., 'Morbid Grief Reactions: A Review of the Literature', Diploma in Psychological Medicine Dissertation, University of London, 1959.

11. SODDY, S., *Clinical Child Psychiatry*, Bailliere, 1960.

Chapter 4d – *Manic Defences*

1. FENICHEL, O., *The Psychoanalytic Theory of Neurosis*, Kegan Paul, 1945.

2. FREUD S., *Mourning and Melancholia*, Standard Edition of Complete Psychological Works, chapter 14, Hogarth Press, 1957.

3. SEGAL, H., *Introduction to The Work of Melanie Klein*, Heinemann, 1964.

4. KLEIN, M., *Contributions to Psychoanalysis*, Hogarth Press, 1954.

Chapter 5 – *The Nature of Schizophrenia*

1. FISH, F. J., *Schizophrenia*, John Wright & Sons, 1962, p. 84.

2. SZASZ, THOMAS, *The Myth of Mental Illness*, Martin Secker & Warburg, 1962.

3. MAYER-GROSS, W., SLATER, E. and ROTH, M., *Clinical Psychiatry*, 2nd edn, Cassell, 1960, p. 290.

4. The Concise Oxford Dictionary.

5. BELL, J. E., 'Recent Advances in Family Group Therapy', *Journal of Child Psychology and Psychiatry*, 1962, 1–15. Excellent source of references.

6. WILHELM, R., and JUNG, C. G., *Secret of the Golden Flower*, Kegan Paul, 1931.

7. FRAZER, J. G., *The Golden Bough*, Macmillan, 1954.

8. FREUD, S., *The Interpretation of Dreams*, trans. Starchey, Allen & Unwin, 1955.

9. PERRY, W., 'Acute Catatonic Schizophrenia', *Journal of Analytical Psychology*, 1957, 2, 137–52.

10. ROSENFELD, HERBERT A., *Psychotic States: A Psycho-analytical Approach*, Tavistock, 1965.

11. (a) TIETZE, T., *Psychiatry*, 1949, 12, 55.
    (b) LIDZ, T., *American Journal of Psychiatry*, 1949, 106, 332.
                     ibid.,   1956, 113, 126.
                     ibid.,   1957, 114, 241.
    (c) ALANEN, Y. O., *Acta psychiatrica et neurologica Scandinavica*, 1958, 33, 124.

12. BATESON, G., JACKSON, D. D., HALEY, J., and WEAKLAND, J.,

'Towards a Theory of Schizophrenia', *Behavioural Science*, 1956, 1, 251.

13. CUMMING, J., and E., *Ego and Milieu*, Atherton or Prentice-Hall, New York, 1962.

14. SARTRE, J.-P., *Words*, Hamish Hamilton, 1964.

15. ibid., p. 59.

16. LAING, R. D., and ESTERSON, A., *Sanity, Madness and the Family*, Tavistock, 1964.

17. ibid., p. 6.

18. LAING, R. D., *The Divided Self*, Tavistock, 1960, p. 36. See also, *The Self and Others*, Tavistock, 1961. Penguin Books 1965.

19. See (18), *The Divided Self*, p. 200. See also cases discussed in (16).

Chapter 6 – *From Custodial Care to Therapy – Physical Treatment*

1. ACKERKNECHT, E. H., *A Short History of Psychiatry*, Hafner, 1959.

2. FISH, F. J., *Schizophrenia*, John Wright & Sons, 1962.

3. SARGANT, W., and SLATER, E., *Physical Methods of Treatment in Psychiatry*, 4th edn, Livingstone, 1963, p. 1.

4. ibid., p. 51.

5. DAVIS, R. D., 'Family Processes in Mental Illness', *Lancet*, 1964, 1, 731–4.

6. (a) *Leucotomy in England and Wales, 1942–54*, H.M.S.O.
   (b) See (2) above.
   (c) Authors still in favour of a modified procedure:
      (i) (3) above.
      (ii) PIPPARD, J., 'Leucotomy in Britain Today', *Journal of Mental Science*, 1962, 249–55.

7. e.g., 'Psychopharmacology: Dimensions and Perspectives', ed. C. R. B. Joyce, Tavistock Publications, London, 1968.

8. SCHON, M., AMDISEN, A. and BASTRUP, P. C., 'The Practical Management of Lithium Treatment', *British Journal of Hospital Medicine*, vol. 6, no. 1, p. 53.

9. 'Long-Acting Phenothiazines', *British Medical Journal*, 1971, 1, 189.

10. *British Medical Journal*, 1971, 1, 557.

11. MOONEY, H. B., 'Pathologic Jealousy and Psycho-chemotherapy', *British Journal of Psychiatry*, 1965, 3, 1023–42.

Chapter 7 – *Social Psychiatry*

1. BROOKE, E. M., *A Cohort Study of Patients First Admitted to Mental Hospitals in 1954 and 1955*, H.M.S.O.

2. CHERRY, C., *On Human Communication*, Massachusetts Institute of Technology Press, U.S.A., 1957.

3. MILLS, E., *Living with Mental Illness*, Routledge, 1962.

4. *A Hospital Plan for England and Wales*, Command Paper 1604, H.M.S.O., 1962.

5. 'Blurred Signposts in Schizophrenia', *British Medical Journal*, 16 March 1963, 695.

6. 'Psychiatric Services in 1975', *Political and Economic Planning*.

7. JONES, K., 'Welfare Work', *New Society*, 10 September 1964.

8. RIN, H. and LIN, T., 'Mental Illness among Formosan Aborigines, as compared with the Chinese in Taiwan', *Journal of Mental Science*, 1962, vol. 108, no. 134.

9. *The Worthing Experiment*, 1 January 1957 – 31 December 1958, South-West Metropolitan Regional Hospital Board, Graylingwell Hospital Occupational Therapy Department.

10. CAUDWELL, C., 'Freud, A Study in Bourgeois Psychology', *Studies in a Dying Culture*, chapter 7, Central Books, 1938.

11. HART, B., *The Psychology of Insanity*, 5th edn, Cambridge University Press, 1957, p. 32.

12. BARTON, R., *Institutional Neurosis*, John Wright & Sons, 1959.

13. e.g. (a) WILMER, H., *Social Psychiatry in Action*, Charles C. Thomas, U.S.A., 1958.

(b) MARTIN, D. V., *Adventure in Psychiatry*, Cassirer, 1962.

(c) CLARK, D. H., 'The Therapeutic Community-Concept, Practice and Future', *British Journal of Psychiatry*, 1965, 3, 947–54.

14. STANTON, A. H., and SCHWARTZ, M. S., *The Mental Hospital*, Basic Books, 1954.

15. GREENBLATT, M., *et al.*, *From Custodial to Therapeutic Patient Care in Mental Hospitals*, Russell Sage, New York, 1955.

16. STANTON, A. H., and SCHWARTZ, M. S., op. cit. p. 326.

17. JOHN, A. L., *A Study of the Psychiatric Nurse*, Livingstone, 1961.

18. JONES, MAXWELL *et al.*, *Social Psychiatry*, Tavistock: Routledge, 1952.

19. DUNHAM, H. W., and WEINBERG, S. K., *The Culture of the State Mental Hospital*, Wayne State University Press, Detroit, 1960.

20. CAUDHILL, W., *The Psychiatric Hospital as a Small Society*, Harvard University Press, 1958.

21. MAIN, T. F., 'The Hospital as a Therapeutic Institution', *Bulletin of the Menninger Clinic*, 1946, 1066–70.

22. TROTTER, W., *Instincts of the Herd*, Benn, 1947, p. 127.

23. CUMMING, J., and E., *Ego and Milieu*, Atherton Press or Prentice Hall, New York, 1962.

24. CAUDHILL, W., REDLICH, F. C., et al., 'Social Structure and Inter-action Processes on a Psychiatric Ward', American Journal of Orthopsychiatry, 1952, 22, 314–34.

25. ATKIN, J., Aspects of Psychotherapy, Livingstone, 1962, pp. 62–3.

26. MARTIN, D. V., Adventure in Psychiatry, Cassirer, 1962, p. 43.

27. See for examples: SOMNER, R. and OSMOND H., 'Autobiographies of Former Mental Patients', Journal of Mental Science, 1960, 648–762, and 1961, 1030–32.

28. BROWN, G. W., 'Length of hospital stay and schizophrenia: A review of statistical studies', Acta psychiatrica et neurologica Scandinavica, 1960, 35, fasces 4, 414–30.

29. BROWN, G. W., Acta psychiatrica et neurologica Scandinavica, 1960, 35, 414.

30. NORTON, A., British Medical Journal, 1961, 1, 528.

31. CAFFEY, E. M., et al., Journal of Chronic Diseases, 1964, 17, 347.

32. WING, J. K., British Journal of Social Clinical Psychology, 1962, 1, 38.

33. BROWN, G. W., 'Experiences of discharged chronic schizophrenic patients in various types of living groups', Millbank Memorial Foundation Quarterly, 1959, 37, 105.

34. (a) BROWN, G. W., et al., Lancet, 1958, 2, 685.
(b) CARSTAIRS, G. M., 'Chronic Mental Illness', quoted in World Health Organization, Public Health Paper 6, 1959.

35. FISH, F. J., Schizophrenia, Bristol Local Medical Committee, 1962, p. 115.

36. GOFFMAN, E., Asylums, Anchor Books, New York, 1961.

37. WING, J K., MONCK, E. M., BROWN, G. W., and CARSTAIRS, G. M., 'Morbidity in the Community of Schizophrenic Patients Discharged from London Mental Hospitals', British Journal of Psychiatry, 1964, 110, 10–21.

38. GRAD, J., and SAINSBURY, P., Lancet, 1963, 2, 544.

39. (a) BROWN, G. W., MONCK, E. M., CARSTAIRS, G. M., and WING, J. K., British Journal of Preventative Social Medicine, 1962.
(b) PARKES, C. M., BROWN, G. W., and MONCK, E. M., British Medical Journal, 1962, 1, 972.
(c) MONCK, E. M., British Journal of Preventative Social Medicine, 1963, 17, 101.
(d) See (37) above.
(e) GOLDBERG, E. M., 'Hospital Work and Family: A Four-Year Study of Young Mental Hospital Patients', British Journal of Psychiatry, 1966, 112, 177–96.

40. RENTON, C. A., AFFLECK, J. W., CARSTAIRS, G. M., and FORREST, A. D., *Acta psychiatrica et neurologica Scandinavica*, 1963, 39, 548.

41. DANIEL, G. R., and FREEMAN, H. L., *The Treatment of Mental Disorder in the Community*, Bailliere, Tindall and Cassell, London, 1968.

42. Department of Health and Social Security, *Psychiatric Hospitals and Units in England and Wales: In-patient Statistics from the Mental Health Inquiry for the Year 1969*, Statistical Report Series, no. 12, H.M.S.O., 1971.

43. 'Psychogeriatric Care', *British Medical Journal*, 1971, 3, 202.

44. JONES, MAXWELL, *Beyond the Therapeutic Community*, London: Yale Press, 1968.

45. ROTH, M., and SCHAPIRA, K., 'Social Implications of Recent Advances in Psychopharmacology', *British Medical Bulletin*, 16, 197–202, September 1970.

46. WING, J. K., and BROWN, G. W., *Institutionalism and Schizophrenia*, Cambridge University Press, 1970.

47. Ministry of Health, *A Hospital Plan for England and Wales*, Cmnd 1604, H.M.S.O., 1962.

48. HAILEY, A. M., *Psychological Medicine*, 1971, 1, 128.

Chapter 8a – *Old Age*

1. KRAPF, E. E., 'On Ageing', *Proceedings of the Royal Society of Medicine*, 46, 957 quoted in *World Health Organization Public Health Paper 16*, 1953, 53.

2. HALSALL, R. W., and LLOYD, W. H., 'Admission of Elderly People to Hospital', *British Medical Journal*, 30 December 1961, 1768.

3. KLEIN, M., 'Mourning: Its Relation to Manic-Depressive States', *Contributions to Psychoanalysis 1921–1945*, Hogarth Press, 1950, p. 319.

Chapter 8b – *Delirium*

1. KENNEDY, A., *Gerontology Clinic*, 1959, 2, 71.

2. MAYER-GROSS, M., SLATER, E., and ROTH, M., *Clinical Psychiatry*, 2nd edn, Cassell, 1960, p. 447.

3. See (2) above, p. 517.

4. ROTHSCHILD, D., quoted in (2) above, p. 515.

5. HENDERSON and GILLESPIE, *Textbook of Psychiatry*, 9th edn, Oxford University Press, 1962, p. 397.

6. 'Current Practice, Today's Drugs. Geriatric Prescribing', *British Medical Journal*, 1 February 1964.

7. See (2) above, p. 530.

Chapter 9 – *Conclusions*

1. ASHLEY MONTAGU, M. F., ed., *The Concept of Race*, Collier-Macmillan, U.S.A., 1964.
2. CARTHY, J. D., and EBLING, F. J., ed., *The Natural History of Aggression*, Academic Press, 1964.
3. HENRY, A. F., and SHORT, J. F., *Suicide and Homicide*, The Free Press, Illinois, 1954.
4. FREUD, S., *An Outline of Psychoanalysis*, Hogarth Press, 1964, p. 7.
5. e.g. Experiments of S. J. Milgram, *Abnormal Social Psychology*, 1963, 67, 371.
6. MARQUIS DE SADE, *Justine*, Spearman, 1964. Note Introduction by A. H. Walton.
7. e.g. FOLKARD, M. S., *A Sociological Contribution to the Understanding of Aggression and its Treatment*, Netherne Hospital, 1961.
8. BROSIN, H. W., ed., *Lectures on Experimental Psychiatry*, University of Pittsburgh Press, U.S.A., 1961.
9. WINNICOTT, D. W., 'Symposium: Training for Child Psychiatry', *Journal of Child Psychology and Psychiatry*, 1963, 4, 85–91.
10. 'Beginning and End of Depression', *British Medical Journal*, 1964, 2, 770–71.
11. (a) CAPLAN, G., *Principles of Preventive Psychiatry*, Tavistock, 1964.
    (b) EISENBERG, L., 'The Strategic Deployment of the Child Psychiatrist', *Journal of Child Psychology and Psychiatry*, 1961, 229–41.
12. *British Medical Journal*, 1964, 2, 1347.

Index